DEPARTMENT OF PUPIL PERSONNEL
617 McKinley Avenue, S.W.
Canton, Ohio 44707

the effective education secretary

Canton City Schools
DEPARTMENT OF PUPIL PERSONNEL
617 McKinley Avenue, S.W.
Canton, Ohio 44707

The Effective Education Secretary

by

jean l. priest
& associates

✦ an etc publication

C | P

Library of Congress Cataloging in Publication Data

Priest, Jean L., 1918-
    The effective education secretary / by Jean L. Priest & associates.

        p. cm. — (Effective school administration series; no. 2) ISBN 0-88280-093-0: $9.95
        1. School secretaries—Handbooks, manuals, etc.
    I. Title II. Series
    LB 2844.4P74 1989   88-6885
    651.3'741—dc19   CIP

No part of this publication may be reproduced or transmitted in any form or by any means, electronic or mechanical, including photocopy, recording, or any information storage and retrieval system now known or to be invented, without permission in writing from the publisher, except by a reviewer who wishes to quote brief passages in connection with a review written for inclusion in a magazine, periodical, newspaper, or broadcast.

Effective School Administration Series - Number Two

Copyright © 1989 by ETC PUBLICATIONS

All rights reserved.

Printed in the United States of America.

contents

FOREWORD

PART I
EFFECTIVENESS PRINCIPLES FOR ALL EFFECTIVE
OFFICE PERSONNEL

ONE
Establishing a Productive Office Climate
1

TWO
Sharpening Your Office Skills
7

THREE
Handling Office Innovations
20

FOUR
Examining Office Ethics
24

FIVE
Improving Rapport with the Boss
28

SIX
Establishing Rapport with the Students, Faculty, and Community
33

SEVEN
Assuming Supervisory Role
35

EIGHT
Using Spare Time Creatively
42

NINE
Responsibility of Administrator
48

TEN
Developing a "YOU"
50

PART II
EFFECTIVENESS PRINCIPLES AT THE EDUCATION SITE

ELEVEN
The Effective Superintendent's Secretary
57

TWELVE
The Effective Assistant Superintendent's Secretary
60

THIRTEEN
The Effective High School Secretary
73

FOURTEEN
The Effective Middle School Secretary
80

FIFTEEN
The Effective Elementary School Secretary
87

SIXTEEN
The Effective Assistant Principal's Secretary
96

SEVENTEEN
The Effective Higher Education Secretary
101

The cartoons in this book are by Mrs. Denis Cummings, Director of Public Information for the Albuquerque Technical-Vocational Institute. She is a former Albuquerque Public Schools teacher.

This book is dedicated to a very effective administrator — my boss. Dr. Noah C. Turpen has been a teacher, a principal, and a superintendent during his career. As he approaches retirement he serves as the Deputy Superintendent for Educational Planning, Research, and Development of the Albuquerque Public Schools, Albuquerque, New Mexico.

Because he is a strong administrator I have always known my area of authority without his having to tell me. My 16 years under his supervision have been the most rewarding of my life.

Jean Priest

*"He" or "she?" the question rose
as I committed thoughts to prose.
Should I call the principal a "he"?
From experience my secretaries are "she."
Reflecting social change with ease
Is difficult — bear with me, please.
The genders may be rearranged —
By second printing all may have changed!*

foreword

How to keep pace with the changing work world is an ever present concern of the modern educational secretary. This book is written with affection and pride of profession in an effort to offer suggestions for refinement of necessary technical and human relations skills, and explores ways in which a secretary can be effective in her job situation and still achieve a sense of personal satisfaction.

The skills necessary to serve the average office now under pressure from all sides are varied and not all concerned with that office's particular salable product.

This book examines in depth suggested methods a secretary can apply working with her employer to build mutual trust and at the same time earn the respect of her coworkers. It touches on the necessary technical skills, and examines ways in which there can be a blending of people with productivity.

In short, this book deals mainly with learning how to face the complexities of the business world; how to establish productive and harmonious job situations; how to be that "Girl Monday through Friday"; and how to create a pleasant, self-satisfying career in the process.

Albuquerque, New Mexico   Jean L. Priest

part I

effectiveness principles for all effective office personnel

by

Jean L. Priest
Albuquerque Public Schools
New Mexico

chapter one
establishing a productive office climate

Does your office smile? The first day as an educational secretary is a sobering experience — one to challenge any smiling face! After spinning through eight long hours of satisfying the demands of others, you'll ask yourself "What have I gotten myself into!" or "Whatever made me think I wanted this job!" Several days later the qualms are over but obviously something must be done to organize your working day; to mend a strained relationship; to re-channel your energies; to cope with the variety of assignments.

Nothing brightens the working day more than to step into a harmonious office. Productivity is at a high level and costly errors are minimal when each occupant of an office carries out his or her particular assignment in an efficient yet relaxed atmosphere.

One determined person can often change the climate of an office, gradually transforming it from a gloomy, unfriendly place to a warm, efficient place where good things happen. You can be that one determined person and your presence in the office can make it the place everyone wants it to be.

Because the job is challenging and where the action is, you'll find it worth the time and talent you devote to it. The successful secretary is wise enough to look first at herself, at her skill in relating to others. She is willing to appreciate the needs and accept the differences of others. Are you?

Improving Your Interpersonal Relationships

Let's examine your motive for becoming an educational secretary. Most of us have a selfish motive for working. We have either found it necessary to earn money or to keep our minds and hands occupied. However, most of us find that as educational secretaries we become so involved with the human side of our role we come to view our positions from the vantage point of what is best for our administrators, how we can best serve their needs, and what is best for the students we serve.

Because you are working it is essential for you to understand what work really is. When we are young and involved with play we most often consider work as something that interferes with what we really want to do — play. It's drudgery! But as we mature we find that work is one activity in which we can completely lose ourselves and not dwell on our problems. When one reconciles one's attitude toward work and approaches it as an expression of love — of oneself — and a necessary function for sound mental health, it becomes acceptable.

After adjusting your mental attitude attempt to establish guidelines for areas of authority from the beginning of your boss-secretary relationship. You'll be interacting with students, teachers, administrators, and the public as well as your employer and without clarification of your scope of authority, problems develop.

The guidelines are simple to establish. Identifying your scope of authority and acting within it is certainly not simple and will be the most difficult thing you will have to master. There are no written rules to follow. The key lies in knowing the philosophy and style of your administrator and how his facet of operation must fit into the overall picture. Working closely beside another person over a period of time is the only sure way to develop an easy, friendly relationship that will carry one through a difficult — sometimes impossible — day.

Nearly every school district has a set of policies established by the board of education, along with the established procedures for implementation. They must be followed to prevent legal problems. Your administrator depends upon you to know those policies and to operate within their framework.

As soon as you have determined and are comfortable within your sphere of influence, you're ready to move ahead with your self-improvement program.

Measuring Your Reliability

Are you known as "The Rock"? If you are not it's time for a change. Probably the most important character trait you'll need in your career as an educational secretary is reliability. Knowing that you can be asked to do something once and it will be done without checking is a source of real satisfaction to your supervisor.

The office is the focal point of any school and to have someone dependable in charge of it is important to students, administrators, teachers, and the patrons of the school district.

The educational secretary will be left alone in the office a great deal of the time because of the number of meetings the average administrator must attend. Over a period of time he will become quite dependent upon you to keep the office and the mechanical functioning of the office rolling along smoothly. The principal of a school will often put a teacher in charge in his absence but the educational secretary is usually the one everyone depends upon when the boss is out of the office, including the teacher who has been placed in the supervisory role.

The administrative secretary in the central office plays the same role in a different setting and the same rules apply in each situation.

There simply are no recognizable steps in the development of reliabilitiy. It is a matter of always keeping your word and having the best interests of the administrator and those you serve in front of you at all times.

The most heartwarming tribute any school secretary can receive is the faith of the students, that she will always be there, that she can be counted on to be of assistance whenever they need her. The admiration of adults is also very important but there is nothing so touching as the gratitude of a young person. The administrative secretary can also find a satisfying niche by constant, unwavering job performance.

Increase Your Bounce

Can you bounce back from disappointments or are you the secretary who cannot function as things go astray? Bouncing well stems from good mental attitude and the ability to accept the inevitable. The inevitable in the school office is never being able to really schedule anything; in the administrative office it's being unable to work on deadline reports without constant interruption.

The ability to accept any situation and not dwell on the frustrations indicates a strong, positive attitude.

View your job with a little detachment and a great deal of humor. Each morning ask yourself what funny thing can possibly happen that day and life becomes a game. Before you open the door, practice stretching your face, widening your eyes, and laughing just a little. You'll find you'll be able to smile readily at the first person you see. Both of you will smile and the day's off to a favorable beginning. As the day progresses you'll find yourself handling difficult situations with ease.

...the ability to accept any situation...

Redoubling Your Curiosity

Physical ills go hand in hand with boredom. Although the job description hardly allows for boredom, there is a certain amount of indifference that filters through any job because of the routine that must be followed. Routine can be comfortable up to a point; beyond that, deadly.

At this point it is necessary for you to inject your own personality into the job. Make something where nothing much exists — if that is the way you are feeling about the job. It's possible! There's a whole world of knowledge out there just for you. Your personality will unfold as you seek knowledge and apply what you've learned to your job situation, and at home.

Someone out there does know how to "build a better mousetrap." What he doesn't know is how to make it work for you — only you know that!

You say you haven't time to read, to take college courses or to improve your educational background, but you have. What you really are lacking if you are telling yourself this is the desire. But once you embark on a self-improvement, self-realization program you'll find it intriguing and fun. You'll find your work enlarging — your horizons stretching. You may suffer frustration when you find your learning processes have become rusty.

Tests can be difficult to cope with after being away from the classroom for a period of several years. The things you'll remember easily in a learning situation are those things you can relate to — things you've experienced.

Begin your improvement program by scanning material that crosses your desk. New concepts of education — or at least old ones dusted off and renewed — abound and one has only to delve a little to be aware of them.

Being curious is being intellectually interested — not snoopy! Your work world will be easier to handle if you can master the terminology of the field of education. Each year finds a plethora of new programs with attendant acronyms and jargon to learn. If you can discuss the pros and cons of practices and theories with your administrator, you will develop a rapport that will help you sense that vague area of authority in which you must function.

The teachers will be pleased if you show an interest in their work and the accompanying problems. The students react warmly to adults who can identify with them and understand their programs.

Being intellectually curious is a rewarding activity. Because the pace of change will continue to accelerate, you *must* develop a wholesome attitude toward it or you'll be a neurotic misfit unable to cope with your work.

In summary, you'll have a productive office climate if you can learn to:

1. Know and like yourself in order to effectively relate to those with whom you work.
2. Know the philosophy and style of your administrator.
3. Be reliable.
4. Handle frustrating situations with good humor.
5. Be interested in the teachers and the students they teach.
6. Be intellectually curious.

chapter two
sharpening your office skills

Effective communication is a refined skill. For many years the mental image of the word "communication" was a written note or letter. The word now carries a much broader connotation involving every possible facet of interaction — voice inflection, eye expressions, body movements, choice of words, written notes, etc. To be always consciously aware of each of these things would practically inhibit one. The mastery should be subtle — part of you!

Working Toward Effective Planned Communication

The school secretary usually feels that *planned* communication is outside the realm of possibility. Things happen too fast with too many people! The professional and conscientious secretary, however, makes a strong effort to avoid confusion and mass misinterpretation by planning whenever possible. The number of interpretations that are given to a seemingly simple notice to the teachers is a source of amazement for those in the office. Equally astounding are the misinterpretations given to a bulletin generating from the superintendent's office.

The time saved by careful construction of a memo or bulletin is well worth the moments involved in planning.

Most of us read and react from our own frame of reference resulting in about as many interpretations as there are people. Fortunately, the well adjusted of our school systems keep the bells ringing.

Daily Bulletins

Preparing the daily bulletin in the average school is a quick way to destroy that feeling of well being you had upon entering the door of the building! So, attitude is the thing!

The secretary who can prepare the bulletin the previous afternoon is better able to construct sentences that make sense. Are you the secretary who must put the bulletin out before classes begin the first thing in the morning? If so, you deserve everyone's sympathy. Early in the morning bedlam usually reigns in the normal school office. To be handed a sheaf of garbled notes only to find after unraveling and typing someone has jammed the duplicating machine and left it for you is enough to make you dissolve in tears. Most things happening around you are necessary and part of the game but others will make you feel as a sailboat buffeted by a stiff breeze. Have you felt this way? Your attitude can save you. Things work out and if you tell yourself that, much wear and tear on your nervous system can be avoided.

If you cannot construct clear, grammatical sentences your first step is obvious. A crash grammar review is indicated.

Short notices are imperative — almost outline style. There are not enough hours in a school day to accomplish everything scheduled for the average classroom. The universal frustration of teachers is lack of time free of paper work to teach. Attempt to convey the message without verbiage.

Most schools have mailboxes eliminating the need to go from room to room. The day will progress more smoothly if everyone is aware of all schedules and announcements. If your administrator reads the announcements over the intercom, keep a complete file of those made if only a sheaf of handwritten notes.

Emergency Notes

Avoid emergency notes whenever possible. Chances for misunderstandings are increased when anything is done on an emergency basis. *Have more than one person read the message before distribution.*

A feeling of apprehension can easily be conveyed to others. Because emotions run high among young people, it's wise to play down tension inducing situations. Should it be necessary to distribute an emergency notice, instruct those hand carrying it to enter quietly and leave without conveying a feeling of urgency. The same applies to an administrative complex.

Memos

Most educational offices have a written memorandum form to be used by all personnel for intra-system correspondence. If your district does not have an accepted form, develop your own and ask your administrator to approve or alter it to his satisfaction. Following is one used by many school districts.

Date

MEMORANDUM
TO: (10 sp.)   Superintendent Smith
FROM: James Brown, Director of Personnel
SUBJECT: State Certification Law

                    Body of memorandum. (Must be carefully planned to avoid misunderstandings.)

SS:jp
Copies to:

Letters

A letter you have typed stands for all the world to see! Never, never send out a business letter containing strikeovers, misspelled words, or hidden meanings. Educational offices should set an example for everyone. In essence, the end products of the entire thrust are knowledge, training, and effective use of both.

If your administrator dictates a letter that is likely to create controversy, ask him if he would prefer a rough draft so you both might see it in print, edit it, and determine if it conveys the intended meaning. Letters can do irreparable damage if anger, disdain, or other emotional reactions are elicited from their contents.

Style manuals can be obtained from any bookstore if you are uncertain about which form of letter to adopt for your own. The full block form is commonly used and easily remembered.

Letter Style

Date

Mrs. Jane Adams, Director
Title I Program
State Department of Education
1801 Capitol Building
Santa Fe, NM 87501

Dear Mrs. Adams:

Body of Letter

Sincerely yours,

Letters should be short and to the point. The amount of paper work crossing the desk of the educational administrator is more than he has time to digest. Most of them will glance at the short ones and put the lengthy publications to one side to "read some day." The letter receives approximately the same treatment, not because of lack of interest but lack of time.

The short, well constructed, and neat letter will receive the attention of the person to whom it's directed.

It is your responsibility to tell your boss if you do not understand what he has dictated. If you do not, chances are that no one else will. Most employers welcome your assistance in helping them operate effectively if it's mutually understood and handled diplomatically. If your intent is free of maneuvering, your efforts will be appreciated.

Often your administrator will correct, add, or alter the letter after you place it on the desk for signature. Don't dwell on the reasons why — his error or yours — save the emotional drain on yourself by retyping. Chances are you'll need the typing practice anyway. Again — attitude is the thing!

Speeches

Many educational administrators are called upon to give speeches at various times. You'll be typing the remarks on 5 x 8 cards or on single sheets of bond paper.

As in letter editing you should be aware of content and connotation. If you do not understand the point your administrator is trying to make, tactfully tell him that there needs to be a little clarification. He will appreciate your efforts — again, if properly approached. Keep a complete file of all his speeches and the place and date delivered.

Strenghtening Your Impromptu Communication

More difficult to cope with is impromptu communication. Face-to-face contact can be a satisfactory or a traumatic experience depending upon your ability to interact successfully with others. All the planning in the world will not completely prepare you for getting along with others. Although as human beings we are all very similar, at the same time we are individuals with various experiences, talents, strengths, and weaknesses.

We cannot plan our encounters or our responses to others. We can, however, be pleasant and strive constantly to rid ourselves of defensive behavior. Students, parents, and fellow employees gravitate toward a person who has learned the value of a smile. Barriers can be lifted with a friendly expression, opening the way to cooperation and understanding.

Enhancing Your Telephone Techniques

One of the most valuable communication skills you can possess is that of handling the telephone. Because the schools work with the most cherished possessions of its patrons — the children — telephone calls are nearly always emotional and can easily be mishandled. The following hints will assist you in making your working day more pleasant:

1. Answer the phone with a smile in your voice. Make that smile genuine. Insincerity is easily detected by the person on the other end of the line and he is insulted immediately.
2. Identify your office and yourself.
3. Employ an imaginative way to find out the nature of the call. For instance, if you cannot connect the caller with your administrator after taking his name and number, ask that person if your administrator will need a file before returning the call. Or, ask if someone can assist in order to avoid the delay. Quite often the caller will divulge the nature of the business to be transacted.
4. If the person calling is angry, let him dissipate his anger by talking to you, always remembering that he is not angry at you but at a situation not of your making. If *you have* angered the caller, offer your apology for having made him angry. If you still feel you are right, try to leave the impression that you regret the unhappiness but that there is another side of the situation. Concede every possible point (and there are always some points upon which you can agree). Agreement has a tendency to lessen the anger of the caller.
5. If you are unable to complete the call before leaving the office at the end of the day, call the person or persons and explain why your administrator is unable to return the call and set up another time. Your concern will be appreciated and will make the call easier for your administrator when he is able to complete the call.
6. Never transfer a call unless absolutely necessary. It is more diplomatic to offer to check out the particular question and return the call yourself.

Developing Memory

The pressures of an educational office make it practically impossible to rely on memory entirely but because a good memory is such a valuable tool every secretary should work on developing one.

A desire to remember must be present before one can be effective in any office situation. Most of us fall into the habit of remembering what we want to and forgetting those things we feel no need for retaining.

Too many message cross the desk of an educational secretary during the course of a normal working day to depend upon memory. However, because of the inaccessibility of most administrators, the task of reviewing and analyzing the order of importance falls on the secretary. More often than not if a secretary fails to deliver a message, the person will contact the administrator outside of the office. Because schools are public institutions, employees are subject to public scrutiny and reaction. Often letters appear in newspapers in the section devoted to letters from the people complaining of real or imagined lack of ability to contact top administrators.

Your concern is to never be guilty of having failed to keep your administrator adequately informed of telephone messages and those personally delivered. You will, of course, occasionally miss one through human error but the amount of confidence your boss places in you will go hand in hand with your ability to deliver sensible messages.

Following are some memory aids:
1. *Mental repetition.* Record *all* messages on a shorthand pad as they come in. Date each morning before starting your day's work. Review all messages several times and when the opportunity arises, carry the pad into the inner office and go over each of the messages with your administrator. Give him the option of placing them in order of their importance. The mental review will assist you in recalling the facts involved. Save the shorthand pads for information. You will find many opportunities to refer to them for names and telephone numbers.
2. *Form a mental image.* As you listen to the message, let your mind work to help you remember. Visualize the school building, the secretary behind her desk, a new addition in progress, or any other association with the caller.
3. *Categorize.* Mentally assess which of your administrator's responsibilities is involved in the message and categorize it mentally as to its importance in his working day.

4. *Record key words* as you go, filling in with additional data as quickly as possible. Never leave a message incomplete except in cases of extreme emergencies. The school secretary will find this the most difficult part of message taking and memory must play a vital role in the process.

Memory tricks will work for you if you develop a desire to remember; give your attention to messages; are observant to everything going on around you; attempt to mentally associate faces, facts, areas; and repeat for retention.

Utter frustration reigns with a mixed up, garbled message because of our natural compulsion to unravel a mystery! Never let your messages be a mystery.

Keeping the Appointment Book

You'll need to call on your sense of humor to keep the appointment book! The modern administrator of a school district of any size must be involved in not only the workings of the schools but must actively participate in state and community affairs. This is a world of group action and because the public tax dollar supports the educational process, citizens are becoming increasingly involved in the decision making.

Only a secretary who has tried to schedule a meeting requiring participation of three or more busy administrators can appreciate the problems encountered in the keeping of the appointment book. Meetings called on the spur of the moment (and there will be many) can cause the loss of valuable minutes because of the excessive number of telephone calls necessary to schedule and then reschedule if there is a breakdown along the way.

Several pointers as listed below will prove helpful in keeping the appointment book:

1. Record all standing appointments that occur daily, weekly, or monthly such as staff meetings, civic commitments, board of education meetings etc.
2. Use pencil because of the number of times you will find it necessary to cancel and reschedule.
3. Note all important dates and times such as graduation, holidays, etc. These can be extensive in the case of the school secretary because of the number of student activities.

Before scheduling meetings involving more than one person, the following hints will save time for you:

1. Check with your administrator to determine those persons who must be in attendance in order to conduct business.

2. Ask if the meeting should be scheduled if certain individuals cannot be present.
3. Obtain alternative dates and hours.
4. Determine the setting for the meeting and an alternative meeting place should the preferred one not be available. Space shortages are a problem in most school systems because of the cost of construction and stringent budgets.

Any meeting you schedule will be more productive if you will give the secretaries as much information as you can concerning the topic for discussion. The administrators involved can make more meaningful contributions if they are well prepared. Your administrator will accomplish more by your foresight.

Always remember to radiate warmth and friendliness on the telephone. The meeting scheduling process is quite often a frustrating one and barriers fall when the channels are open for good communication.

Before you leave the office for the night, remind your administrator of an evening meeting or an early morning meeting the next day. Place all material he will need before the opening of your office the next morning beside a regular established place if you leave the office before he is free.

Remember — the appointment book can be as confining as a prison cell to your administrator. Be an expediter — not a jailer!

Coordinating and Channeling Material Through the Office

In many administrative complexes there is a game administrators play — "hide it from our secretaries!" Fortunately it's an activity completely free of malice, but the end result can result in hours of wasted time. Written materials are carried into the staff and cabinet meetings, assigned to one or more of the administrators for handling, seeming never to be found again! When someone receives the subject, all administrators remember having seen the material and just know that their secretaries can produce it from their files. At this point an endless search operation between secretaries and administrators begins.

Any secretary feels the sting of not being able to immediately come forth with the necessary papers from her files.

In the schools principals have difficulty because teachers and students often give them papers or notes in the hallway that are lost or misplaced through the process of functioning for several hours before returning to the office.

Keeping track of all important papers is not a little task for a secretary. An employee new to a job can only speculate as to the importance of documents. But if the desire for top performance is present, a little extra effort and homework will facilitate the categorizing and handling of the paper flow.

Most educational offices have access to photocopying machines which makes the job easier. Before putting important material on your administrator's desk, make a copy for your files. Record where you send reports, questionnaires, etc. if you send them outside of your office for disposition.

Because many papers, letters, magazines, newsletters, etc. can be read at odd moments, a good secretary will sort the material for her boss before placing on the desk. One time saving method is to label letter file folders as follows:

(Type label on each folder)

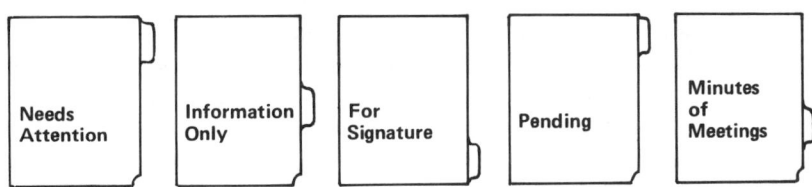

Filing in the proper folder serves as a memory trick because of the decision making process involved. Your administrator will soon form the habit of checking the folders each day to see what has been added. It is one small way of saving time. Occasionally you'll be in a quandary concerning the importance of a letter or report. The best way to handle it is to place it in the folder marked "Attention." As you become increasingly familiar with the job, you will find it easier to sort for the proper folder. Your administrator, always pressed for time, will quickly check the "Attention" and "Signature" folders saving the others for later.

Most administrators need a certain amount of material close at hand. Budget material, school bond issue information, statistics for the school district, class size, teaching stations, along with information pertinent to his job specialization should be at this fingertips. Budget restrictions quite often prevent ordering sophisticated filing equipment. An inexpensive set of files can be developed for the upper, lefthand corner of his desk by obtaining three metal file cases for upright storage of heavy cardboard file folders with angular celluloid tabs. Alphabetize them and he will soon develop a sense of pride being able to work at his desk without constantly interrupting you.

If your administrator is a school principal, the folders should contain information and labeled "To Discuss at Faculty Meeting," "To Discuss with Superintendent." "Teaching Stations," etc. Should your administrator be one of district office level there should be a folder "To Discuss with Superintendent," "To Disuss with Board," "District Statistics," etc.

The same type of filing system on the right- or lefthand corner of your desk will save time for you. Files such as reports with deadlines, pay period time records, employee lists (for smaller systems), your current committee assignments are examples.

Clearing Your Administrator's Desk

If your administrator is one who is inclined to write short messages of one or two words on note pads, file folders, envelopes, etc. that soon become lost on the desk, fasten the note to an 8½ x 11 sheet of paper and place in the "Pending" folder. Once a week ask him to review these notes and the material in the folders with you. Carry your shorthand pad (the one by the telephone) and record the disposition of each letter or report. If you are merely to file, place in a stack before you and record the disposition of the balance of the papers.

If you ask to go over everything to help ease his mind about the amount of work yet to do, your thoughtfulness will be appreciated and you will be able to easily dispose of much of the load. Not having enough time to devote to the reports and paperwork of an educational office is a constant source of frustration to an administrator.

Call on your imagination to find effective ways to channel the paper through your office.

In summary, develop ways to record, circulate, and retain all important information flowing through your office.

1. Photocopy one each of all important material that is likely to be carried out of your office. Ask for *two* copies of reports that are directly related to the operation of your office.
2. Find a method that will work for you and your administrator to keep all pertinent information close at hand to minimize interruptions.
3. Develop a set of desk files for his personal use.
4. Collect all notes on slips of papers, envelopes, etc. and tape to 8½ x 11 sheets of paper to prevent their being lost.
5. Schedule a time to review the paper work on the desk with your administrator.

...collect all notes for filing...

chapter three
handling innovations

Young people generate change. Your ability to cope with the forces will determine your success working in the educational world — elementary, junior high, high school, college or university, or whatever level of involvement. Not all change is good but it is a very real part of your career and must be faced realistically. Your ability to interact with young people — to accept them as they are without being shocked or projecting a desire to make them over — is a necessary character trait.

Facing Changes

Change is always with us. Have the perception of timeliness you'll need to function in a changing society. Be friendly with the present but always remember there is a past and there will be a future. Not much can be done with the past except benefit from its lessons. The present requires about as much of you as you can give.

Don't resist the future. After all, it's one minute away from the present. It has been said that we age not from years but from our loss of awareness.

An effective educational secretary is cognizant of the past, aware of the future, and completely at home in the present. She is open to experience — good or not so good!

The signature is scarcely dry on a memo before the content becomes out-dated. Assume from the outset that the process used today will not be exactly the same as the one to be used next. Most processes improve with time. The most important thing to remember is that the school systems of our Nation represent every conceivable facet of our society and are therefore complex. Nothing is simple; everything must be designed for that complexity. Breathe your sigh, if you must, but organize your materials and thoughts for the specific task at hand. Remember always that teachers, administrators, students — everyone — will cooperate if you approach them in a positive, helpful manner at all times, not just when you want something from them. In every office setup of more than three employees there are always two or three who must be continually prodded — who can never quite meet a deadline. Acknowledge that fact and schedule your work around them.

The college or university secretary works in a slightly different atmosphere. Many students are trying their wings for the first time, are weaning away from their parents. They are in an experimental stage of development with many of them making major decisions on their own for the first time in their lives. A great deal of empathy is required on the part of the educational secretary in such cases. Some of the mistakes they make are traumatic. The secretary or cashier who has the unhappy lot of facing a student who has failed to arrange for tuition payment or who has failed a course through lack of self-discipline and must "face the music" from home, must have reserves of empathy.

The changes, demonstrations, and destructive forces generated from a campus of higher learning are a part of the existence of such a secretary and she must be prepared to live with them.

Maintaining an Open Mind

Keeping pace with change and all of the problems connected with it can only be accomplished through maintaining an open mind. A narrow mind warps — distorts your sense of fair play — and in general makes you miserable.

Adjusting, Assisting, and Assessing Innovations

Adjusting to new ways of doing things requires your believing that there are better ways of getting the job done and if you can't actually assist in their development don't stand in the way of those who can. Always be willing to cooperate and encourage anyone capable of designing a new and better process. Quite often your talents and enthusiasm will be all that is needed to mean the difference between success and failure. Be known for your positive attitude and never be guilty of being rigid and uncompromising.

Nearly every innovation has something of value to offer if not completely acceptable to those for whom it was designed. Be willing to experiment and if a new process is not completely successful in your operation, find the positive points and put them to use. If the innovation is not faster, is not simpler, and does not contribute

required data to the system more efficiently than previous methods, it will be abandoned. Your lack of enthusiasm, along with others, will contribute to that.

In summary:
1. Remember lessons of the past, enjoy the present, and anticipate the future.
2. Don't resist change; be shockproof!
3. Have an open mind and appreciate the freedom it offers.
4. Use innovations to your advantage.
5. Above all, be supportive and enthusiastic.

chapter four
examining office ethics

Values that were once a part of many of us are being shaken by social forces leaving uncertainty in their place. Administrators everywhere are faced with a new breed of employee — one who is seldom interested in protecting the image of his employer. Because the working world of the average school administrator is hectic and enervating it is important that he have supportive, interested, and highly trained employees backing him at all times.

Keeping Confidences

Although schools are public institutions and their operation must be open to public inspection there are countless confidential files that must be kept as personal files unless permission is given by the individual to disclose their contents. Attendance records tell a story — cumulative folders are revealing. A grade record charts a student's progress — or lack of it.

Everyday you will find yourself involved in situations that require judgment and confidentiality. Respect the privacy of others. Refrain from idle talk. If you cannot, you'll soon have a reputation among the students and the faculty that will drop you from the "effective" to the "ineffective" ranks. No longer can your boss discuss confidential matters with you; in fact, there can be no more sharing at that point.

Respecting Individual Differences

One of the most difficult lessons in life to learn is that although we are very much alike we are at the same time different from each other. Each of us is a sum total of our inheritance, our environment, and our experience. We act and react from our own frame of reference often creating "sticky" situations. Recognize the differences in people and what makes them "tick." Most of the time the people you work with will be predictable but occasionally the behavior pattern will drastically change and be upsetting to you. Develop an attitude adjustment capability and you'll be able to cope with any situation.

One of the most common differences encountered in a group of people working together is that of "day people" and "night people." Many of us function better during the early hours of the day while others can't function efficiently until afternoon. Their productivity level is best from 4:00 p.m. to midnight. Working together during the afternoon of each day can be a traumatic experience for everyone if the individual differences are not recognized and appreciated. Tease each other gently, if you are able to, at the same time being considerate of each other. Let the early birds run the forenoon and the late bloomers dominate the afternoon. This cannot always be done, but should be done if possible.

Practicing the Golden Rule

Most of us are taught from early childhood to appreciate the dignity of our fellow man, but the pressures of a school office tend to make those staffing it momentarily forget the lessons they've learned.

We age gracefully if we can accept the unique qualities of those around us and learn to harmoniously interact with them. Losing your temper can only damage you. It upsets your body both emotionally and physically and creates a negative reaction from those around you. However, losing your temper is not to be confused with taking a stand for what you consider to be right!

A school full of young people at various stages of maturity requires an endless amount of patience on the part of everyone and the easiest human relations gimmick to remember is the Golden Rule. It preserves the dignity of the human soul.

Too often we are guilty, as adults, of talking down to young people, embarrassing them in front of others, and instantly categorizing them. Practice that Rule as you work with them — whatever level of maturity — remembering always that they have feelings such as we, plus that painful vulnerability accompanying younger years.

As the students seek your attention, look each one in the eye and search for any kind of beauty — superficial or soul — and you'll discover yourself caring about preserving the dignity of that individual. Too often the maladjusted of our world overbalance the

...one common difference is that of "day people" and night people...

adjusted by the attention they demand. Fortunately, we are awakening to the needs of the few but, unfortunately, the trauma involved in the process has a tendency to create less than a desirable effect.

In the long run each of us can only be held accountable for our own actions. What safer guideline can we follow than the Golden Rule? Its value can never be measured in depth or distance.

Appreciating Privileges

Appreciation takes many forms with all of us. Sometimes we openly express our thankfulness when we are given an unusual privilege such as unscheduled time off, while other times we show our appreciation by not taking advantage of a situation. The latter works like magic in an office situation. Just knowing that you can be given a little leeway and you'll not overdo it will encourage your employer to relax and grant favors now and then.

The coffee break is the most abused of the privileges given to any office employee but is a necessary part of the working day. School secretaries often must forego the coffee break simply because the pressure of her day will make it impossible. Her principal often sends her home a few minutes early after a particularly frustrating day to compensate. The administrative secretary in the central office must schedule her break to fit the schedule of her administrator and the secretary who insists on leaving the office for her coffee at a set time each day is shortsighted. The efficient administrative secretary will schedule her break between appointments when her employer is occupied with a meeting or interview behind closed doors. Her absence is not so obvious at such a time.

Examining Office Ethics involves:
1. Keeping confidential information confidential.
2. Respecting individual differences and realizing that life is more fun because we are not all carbon copies of each other.
3. Making your Golden Rule at least 13" long.
4. Not expecting privileges — respecting them.

chapter five
improving rapport with the boss

The stress facing the average educational administrator is incredible. In order to help him face these pressures it is important to develop rapport if you do not already have it.

Working side by side eight hours a day makes it necessary to be comfortable — at ease — with each other. Occasionally two people have instant rapport but usually it develops with a passing of time and a sharing of experiences. If it does not develop within a reasonable period, examine your working relationship in the light of its effectiveness. Perhaps some habit pattern that can be altered or abandoned is the stumbling block.

Know your boss, what motivates him, and what makes him effective in his job.

Take a moment, and it may only be a moment or two at a time, to discuss educational philosophies with him. There are countless opportunities in the course of running your office to discuss your work. Student demonstrations, teacher negotiations, innovative programs, etc. provide experiences you can share. When you ask a question, stop to listen and do very little talking. You boss' philosophy toward his work will emerge and you'll be able to run his office the way he wants it run. A great deal of your training evolves this way.

Respect his whims and recognize that they are a part of his personality and help make an individual. Remember, like you he is saved from being a carbon copy of others by his whims or eccentricities. Usually if you accept him this way your role will be much easier and you'll be working under fewer pressures. If you cannot accept him the way he is, start looking for another job.

Facing Office Pressures

Living with pressure is easier if you've had adequate sleep and know how to rest your body and mind as needed. Develop a daily

..know him and accept his eccentricities...

schedule involving everything you do and maintain it over a long period of time to determine the number of hours of sleep you require and the added amount of rest period you need during the day. Without being a slave to the pattern, attempt to follow the schedule. You'll pace yourself in such a way that you'll be able to face the day and what it brings.

Your attitude in the office will nearly always determine the treatment you will receive from your boss. If you can handle the pressure without losing your temper, you automatically lessen his pressures and that is one of your main functions as an educational secretary.

Deadlines generate pressure. It is important to analyze the demands of society to understand why the reports and surveys are increasing in quantity and complexity. Accept the inevitable deadlines, realizing that you'll meet them somehow. You will find that this acceptance will ease the pressure.

Sharing Employee Pressures

Because more often than not your employer's time will be scheduled too full to be available when needed by everyone under his immediate supervision it will be your responsibility to keep situations and tempers from reaching the danger point. *Never* imply that it is impossible to see your administrator. Leave a ray of hope in their minds if it is only to schedule them for a moment between appointments or on his way in and out of the office. Whether or not the appointment actually takes place is irrelevant. You have satisfied their emotional needs. Although some of the contacts are seemingly not necessary, there is a morale factor present. There are times when just a word of encouragement or even acknowledgement from one's superior will serve an emotional need. Your administrator is aware of his responsibility in this respect and although it adds to his pressures, he recognizes your role to provide the employee an opportunity to fulfill that need. There will be times when you'll be tempted to judge whether or not an appointment is really necessary but it is wise to allow your boss to make such a decision. Your area of authority is involved in this situation and unless you are absolutely certain of your administrator's reaction don't make that judgment.

If you are in an office with one or more employees, it is most important to keep the peace among yourselves. You'll find it's difficult enough to handle the pressures from the outside. If you are fortunate, you'll have a harmonious atmosphere. If not, it will be a challenge to you to achieve it and keep it that way. It's your responsibility because you want to be effective in your job. Only *you* can accomplish that. If you interact harmoniously, the pressure on your administrator is diminished, thereby automatically easing yours.

Handling Ticklish Situations

There are times when you must run interference for your boss. There are usually people he avoids, either from personality conflict or other personal reasons. It will be your lot as his secretary to delay the appointment without offending them. If you are dealing with someone not under his immediate supervision, find a tactful way to find out if that person is following the proper channels of organization. It is a waste of everyone's time and energy if the person has bypassed all those who should be acknowledged of the appointment. If this is the case, you will increase the pressure of your administrator because he must adhere to the lines of authority to avoid dissatisfaction among his peers.

Polishing His Image

The impression of your administrator which you leave with your coworkers and the public is most important and thus should be an area of concern for you. There are countless ways one can undermine another without being cognizant of having done so. Don't be guilty of a condemning shoulder shrug or a raised eyebrow.

Be supportive of your administrator and never project the impression either on the job or outside the office that he is lacking in the qualities necessary for a strong manager. If you cannot be supportive of your administrator, then you should look for another job.

Priorities for Polishing His Image

1. Getting him to his appointments on time with the necessary materials in his possession.
2. Assisting him to prepare all reports expected of him and to meet the deadlines set.
3. Trying to be neat, orderly, and accurate in your work. He benefits as a result.
4. Finding imaginative and tactful ways to cover up for him should he fail to return a telephone call or miss a scheduled appointment.
5. Exhibiting a willingness to learn everything about your job

and progress to greater responsibilities under his supervision. The more trained you are the more effective he seems to others.
6. Accepting his decisions in good faith and avoiding discussing them with coworkers.

You'll be more comfortable working with your administrator if you can:
1. Work to eliminate any stumbling block that might be causing communication problems between you.
2. Know him and accept his eccentricities — the whims that make him an individual.
3. Strive to understand his world and his philosophy.
4. Learn to face his office pressures.
5. Share his employee pressures.
6. Run interference for your boss — diplomatically.
7. Polish his image both on the job and outside the office.

chapter six
establishing rapport with the students, faculty, and community

Although this era of negotiated agreements has made it more difficult to interact harmoniously with school faculties, an effective secretary still has an opportunity to establish rapport with most of her teachers. The unwillingness of some teachers to extend themselves beyond the contract makes a less than satisfactory situation. When teachers are reluctant to do many of the tasks to be done around a school, the principal often instructs the secretary to withdraw services she might ordinarily render the faculty. However, the wise secretary will do everything she can to keep the relationships happy and productive. A feeling of camaraderie will usually develop between the office staff and the teachers if those involved make an extra effort to work together. Most teachers still are dedicated and conscientious notwithstanding the advent of negotiated labor-type contracts.

Students reflect the changing times also with some displaying a general indifference to the processes of learning. Fortunately, there are many earnest and ambitious young people who make the rendering of service a little more palatable than it would otherwise be.

A genuine interest and involvement in their programs and activities usually is all that is necessary to establish understanding with the students. Secretaries in the secondary schools nearly always become enthusiastic about the student academic and athletic contests.

Too often the school office sees only the troublesome students — the policy violators. It is not impossible, however, for the secretary who has been patient with a chronic "office sitter" to see that student become president of the chamber of commerce in later years. There are those whose emotional problems are too complex, of course, but the majority of the students are captivating to be around.

Community involvement is a way of life for the modern school system and every employee must adjust to that fact. Education systems are expensive and require a large portion of the tax dollar. With each passing year more and more citizens are becoming interested in the educational process. It has been said that "Involvement is pooled ignorance" and frustration builds in the face of ignorance. Certainly, involvement also can result in positive outcomes, and often does. The secretary often is the first contact a patron of the school district makes and her attitude sets the tone for the involvement. An awareness of community developments can be of great assistance to the secretary as she attempts to serve. For some reason unknown to educational employees the public looks to the schools to solve most of the ills of society. Scan the morning paper and you'll be able to anticipate many of the telephone calls for the day. Don't be defensive when the calls come in. Instead, courteously receive complaints and suggestions and assure patrons solutions to problems are being worked on. Direct callers to appropriate individuals when indicated.

Rapport builds gradually in most cases but you can hasten its course in the following ways:
1. Attempt to cross the barrier between you and the teachers if they hide behind the negotiated agreement. Be willing to go that "second mile."
2. Be genuinely interested in the activities and programs of the students.
3. Be patient with the chronic "office sitters."
4. Be aware of community developments and how they affect the schools.
5. Remember that most people who contact the schools do so because they are interested in the educational process. They are concerned with problems that develop and desire to find solutions.

chapter seven
assuming supervisory role

Working as a supervisory secretary requires special skills and a deep reservoir of patience. Should you be asked to work in such a capacity it becomes necessary for you to examine the categories of the leadership function to determine whether or not you can meet the demands.

Do you like working with others or are you a "loner"? Do you care about your district, your system, the job, the people? Are you loyal and supportive of those for whom you work? Ask yourself if you are pressure oriented. Will you "blow" under stress? Are you able to accept the challenge of problem solving, the pain of growth and innovation? Can you do the job and still be true to yourself and what you believe — is it your "cup of tea"? Can you remain cheerful and optimistic in the face of frustration? Can you bounce back from disappointments? All of these are underlying factors that will affect your performance as a supervisor. Proceed if you are comfortable with these things.

Preparation for Supervision

When you develop, establish, and define goals in your own mind, the job of supervising others is easier. What do you hope to accomplish with those you will be directing? Do you have common goals? Until you identify your own, it will be difficult to establish consensus with others. After establishing your own, it is essential to confer with those you will be leading to discuss the things you want to achieve with a combined effort. Underlying all discussion must be the end result required by the administration and the board of education.

Examine your own need to control. If you have an unmet emotional need, the inclination to overcontrol often becomes more dominant than it otherwise would. *Power is corrupting and its abuse renders you ineffective with those around you.*

Work to create an atmosphere of productivity. Harmony is an intangible and must be prevalent for top efficiency in any office. Working together in harmony comes with experience — of trial and error.

Physical conditions in an office can be controlled and an effective supervisory secretary should work to have them as ideal as possible. High on the list of priorities is temperature, whether heat or air conditioning. While heat is enervating, extreme cold is equally uncomfortable and employees who are constantly concerned about the temperature of the office are not fully concentrating on the job at hand.

Wall paint can affect the employee. Light shades of green, pale yellow, light coral, and light pink usually produce the desired effect in contrast to heavy, darker colors. Emphasis should be placed on creating an illusion of space if the office area is not large. Many school districts are not able to construct enough office space for their needs due to budgetary restrictions.

Adequate and well spaced electrical outlets are essential, keeping extension cords at a minimum. Desks should be placed for proper lighting.

Ideally, each employee in an office staffed by several should have 50 sq. ft. of working space including filing cabinets. If this cannot be, 30 sq. ft. is the bare minimum. The noise level is increased when several typewriters and telephones are too close together. Fatigue results from too much noise and fighting unsatisfactory working conditions throughout the working day, and we are all inclined to react to the personal problems of each other when in too close a physical proximity — our moods "rub off" on each other.

While these items seem rather insignificant, they contribute in a very real way to the smooth functioning of an office and therefore *are* important and should be considered before you begin any kind of supervisory work.

Assignment of Duties

In many office situations one can find an inequitable division of duties and an accompanying undercurrent of dissatisfaction among employees.

The executive secretary seldom follows the same type of routine as does the secretary in the personnel or accounting divisions. Her work, by nature, cannot always be scheduled and varies a great deal.

Because the work cannot be preplanned, her task is as difficult as that of the clerk who sits behind a mountain of detailed paper work. An effective supervisory secretary will be certain that those who are under her supervision clearly understand the nature of her role as a supervisory secretary. Otherwise subordinates may wrongfully conclude, because she has few routine tasks, that she is not carrying her fair load. Nothing could be further from the truth!

If you have the authority to assign tasks, ascertain the talents — the special skills — of those with whom you will be working. Try to fit their strengths with the jobs you will be asking them to do rather than assigning a project to someone who is weak in the skills needed to perform the job. It is seldom possible to divide the workload equally for that reason. Everyone wants to excel and should be given the opportunity to do so.

Always set aside enough time when assigning duties to clarify what you expect from those under your supervision. Nothing is more frustrating than having a job to do without really knowing how to do it or what's required of you. Well defined procedures and goals permit the employees to function effectively and smoothly. Make it possible for your coworkers to admit that they do not understand if they do not. Don't be guilty of wasting their valuable time with wondering what you mean. Outline in your mind what you want to accomplish before attempting to assign work to others. The good supervisor does not say "I would rather do it myself." She trains others.

Establishing the Team Concept

The employee morale of your office will be good if you follow sensible assignments and clarification of duties with your personal availability. The work flow will not be interrupted if you are there to answer questions when they arise. There may be one or two individuals who will have questions that seem unimportant to you but handle them cheerfully because a morale boost may be all that is really needed.

Involve those with whom you work in decision making whenever possible. There will be much you cannot share but there will be countless opportunities to open the door for effective communication and a building of trust. Employees who trust their immediate supervisor and each other function smoothly as a team. Knowledge of how to perform the job at hand, an opportunity to provide input, and a feeling of being supported makes for an ideal working situation for any employee.

...in many office situations one can find an inequitable division of duties...

Anticipating change and preparing those under you for it will be a very valuable function in your role as a supervisor. It is not always possible to forecast social changes that affect the running of an educational office but there are signs that when added together a trend is indicated. When you become aware of an impending change, begin to expose the employees to the ways in which their jobs will be affected. Job insecurity is a frightening specter and employee resistance occurs when one attempts to change a procedure too quickly. Everyone immediately feels their job is threatened. The wise supervisor lays the groundwork well in advance of an impending change.

There will be times when you will find it necessary to "go to bat" for someone under your immediate supervision as there are many things you will observe that may never come to the attention of your employer. Those you supervise will have a tendency to be loyal to you if they feel your support of them.

Regulating the Office Work Day

Always be fair in planning the office day. Everyone appreciates a small break in the morning and another in the afternoon and usually function better if given them. Some want coffee while others prefer to take a brisk walk around the building. Provide the opportunity for every employee to have such breaks and encourage each one to take them, making certain that no one abuses the privilege. Allow for flexibility because of the differences in work load and individual preference. Should there be a conflict in scheduling, make the decision yourself if the conflict cannot be removed by working with those involved.

Recognize that everyone will need to make an occasional personal telephone call, a visit to the doctor or dentist, or run a personal errand. Work within the policy of the district and treat any abuses of the privileges expeditiously and firmly. Don't let one offender ruin the privileges of the others.

Whenever possible hire substitutes for those on vacation or out of the office for medical reasons. There will be some desks that do not require substitutes and those that must have a steady work flow. It will be your responsibility to plan for the absences whatever the reasons may be.

As a supervisor you must hold the reins and be candid about what you expect from those you supervise. You will not always be popular but those who make decisions must recognize that it is not a popular process.

Refrain from taking sides in an employee disagreement, and there will be disagreements. Never discuss one employee with another. Socializing with one of your employees after hours leads to trouble and is a "refrain from" of supervision. The human tendency is to expect favors from friends — something you can't grant as an office manager.

Your success as a supervisor will depend upon whether or not you can find the cause of trouble spots, resolve them, and not merely react to symptoms of trouble.

Evaluating Employee Performance

As a supervisory secretary you will be asked to evaluate those under your direction. The first person to evaluate is yourself. Can you evaluate others impartially? Have you been able to utilize their talents without trying to manipulate them? Have you assigned others tasks you are not willing to perform yourself? Have you listened *and heard* what they have tried to say to you? Have you accepted the responsibility for your actions and the action of others under you? Have you considered the burden of responsibility you have delegated and the nature of it? Have you assessed the workload and equalized it during the year insofar as possible? Have you been realistic in the deadlines you have established?

Always evaluate an employee's performance — positively using only constructive criticism. Work on an individual basis with the employees under your supervision in determining how things might be done more efficiently. Never approach a problem from a negative point of view. Evaluation should be a tool for both the supervisor and employee to use for better, more productive working relationships.

On-the-Job Growth

Encourage on-the-job growth and whenever possible promote those who qualify for promotion. Recognize those who achieve through extra effort. Growth on the part of those you supervise often occurs as a natural outgrowth of your attitudes and conduct. Project a progressive, professional image rather than an indifferent one.

In short:
1. Examine the categories of the leadership function to see if you are comfortable with them.
2. Establish personal and common goals for the office.

3. Try for the best possible physical working conditions for those under your supervision.
4. Assign duties as equitably as possible utilizing the talents of your staff. Clarify what you expect from each one.
5. Hold the reins.
6. Be available to answer questions.
7. Support your employees whenever their performance is called into question if they deserve it.
8. Involve those under you in the decision making process whenever possible.
9. Regulate the personal privileges of your employees in a practical, humane way.
10. Assess and equalize the workload as changes occur.
11. Do not assign tasks to others that you are not willing to undertake yourself.
12. Do not react to symptoms of trouble. Define and correct the causes.
13. Refrain from taking sides in an employee disagreement.
14. Refrain from discussing one employee with another.
15. Listen and *hear*. Communicate.
16. Evaluate honestly and impartially.
17. Encourage on-the-job growth and promote from within the unit whenever possible. Recognize a job well done.

chapter eight
using spare time creatively

Never be guilty of wasting time — one of life's most precious gifts! Should you find yourself with a few extra moments on the job, an excellent way to utilize them is to work on development of an inservice training program for secretarial/clerical personnel.

School administrators are nearly always receptive to the idea of training for their personnel but often do not have the staff and time to conduct the training programs. If you can design a program and present it effectively, you can be displaying your talents and at the same time be serving your administration.

Remember that an on-going training program will be successful only if it is needed in the first place. If the need exists, develop a plan that outlines the purpose of the training and implementation of the plan.

Developing the General Purpose of an Inservice Program

In most cases the employees need to be updated in their skills and new employees need to be trained and reinforced. The following are recognized purposes for training programs:
1. Training facilitates the work flow by eliminating unnecessary questions.
2. The training creates awareness of work done by others.
3. Training done by employees reduces the cost of the inservice effort.
4. Inservice workshops improve rapport between the employees and creates an understanding of the total job situation.

Appointment of Committee

The chairman of the committee must be a dedicated, enthusiastic person who will follow up on assignments and is willing to carry on the mechanical function necessary to any on-going program. You can be that person! The committee itself should be composed of a representative from each area of operation and should be the person who actually works with the personnel in the school offices. Include a member from the highest level of operation, from the personnel division, finance division, data processing center, instructional division, maintenance and operations, supplies and textbooks, and the media center. A large committee functions better and if handled right becomes a training ground for several inservice leaders. The committee members can be given the responsibility of handling a meeting when the chairman is not available to carry through a scheduled assignment.

Development of a Schedule

The responsibility of each committee member is to survey the problems in the particular phase of operation involved and identify the pressing ones. As the survey is made at the various levels, a magic "brainstorming" takes place.

The committee must refine the material gathered as there will be a duplication of concerns. After gathering the problems of the field, the key divisions of the system should be consulted to determine changes in procedures. This can be done by the members on the committee representing the divisions.

Next comes the framework for the meetings such as the days, hours, and types of meetings. The scheduling of workshops must be studied to allow for adequate break periods with enough time devoted to actual workshop content. There should be a good mixture of sitting, standing, and moving around.

The most difficult part of the planning will be the selection of subject matter and instructors for the workshops. The topics must be timely, interesting, and needed by the participants. It is essential to have excellent speakers and leaders as it is difficult to maintain excellence. The committee has the responsibility of long-range planning with a definite goal in mind.

There should be a training of new employees before school begins with an enrichment workshop for experienced personnel.

Divide the two and schedule on different days. The personnel new to the system should be trained in a full-day session with the first half consisting of explicit training on the use of requisitions; on the preparation of the attendance reports; on the ordering of supplies, textbooks, and equipment; on learning the use of the handbooks on policies and procedures, etc. The last half of the day should be on the job site such as the elementary school office. The elementary school trainer on the committee should take those who are new to the elementary school office into the school and demonstrate how the school office is run.

The new employees can also participate in the enrichment sessions and usually are interested in doing so.

A session to correct and reinforce procedures for the new employees should be held about six weeks after the start of the school term. The same employees should again be brought together to be trained in the closing of the school year procedures approximately two months before the end of the term.

Secretaries and clerks who actually receive the reports of the school secretaries or supporting services personnel should be the ones who do the training in the workshops. Two results will emerge: 1) the helper and receiver will become acquainted; and 2) effective working relationships are established.

Lawyers, psychologists, personnel officers of corporations, etc. are often willing to serve educational institutions without reimbursement and make excellent resource persons for instructors. Teachers will also donate their time and talents to inservice training classes on occasions.

Assignments of Committee Members

The chairman (and it could be you) should divide committee assignments and rotate responsibilities to train several to carry on the work of the committee in the absence of the chairman. Each committee member provides input to the training effort and lends a variety of skills.

Physical and Program Arrangements

Assign responsibility for the following after the program content has been determined:
  A. *Registration.* The person serving as registration chairman should recruit adequate help and coordinate their duties.
  1. The placement of the tables, the chairs, the ventilation and open space for flow of traffic should be checked well in advance of the scheduled meeting.
  2. Order signs for all necessary information such as location of meeting rooms, small group meetings, etc.
  3. Collect and collate hand-out material.
  4. Obtain money in logical denominations for making change.
  5. Collect supplies such as felt point pens, pencils, pins, paper clips, rubber bands, masking tape, etc.

6. Type name tags in primer type or write in large handwriting to facilitate reading.
B. *Hostesses.* A friendly greeting will start any meeting off happily. The chairman in charge of the hostesses should:
1. Assign one or two secretaries to greet the participants as they arrive and to answer questions (leaving those assigned to the registration table free to carry on with the registration.)
2. Assign one person to assist the principal speakers or leaders with any needs they might have at the last minute.
3. Strive to keep a mixing process underway so there can be an active interchange of ideas.
C. *Audiovisual Arrangements.* School districts of any appreciable size have an audiovisual department. If there is a secretary in that department, she should be a member of the committee and should be involved in arranging for the equipment. She should:
1. Arrange for screens, microphones, or projectors.
2. Check wiring and have extension cords if needed.
3. Check projector in advance.
4. Check to see if room can be darkened for movies or slides.
5. Stand by to troubleshoot during the meeting.
6. Collect and return all equipment to the audiovisual department.
D. *Meal Functions and Coffee Breaks.* Appoint someone to be in charge of these functions should you have them included in the meeting. Allow adequate time for serving and restroom breaks.
E. *Evaluation.* One member of the committee can be in charge of designing, circulating, and collecting the evaluation sheet. The meetings should meet the needs of the participants and the evaluation sheet serves the committee in determining this.

The chairman coordinates the work of the various subchairmen and can increase the chances for success by:
A. Developing handout sheets for each workshop such as zip code and abbreviations of States; often misspelled words; organizational charts, etc.
B. Sending out notices and reminder notices of the scheduled meetings, making certain that each notice carries the coordinated signatures of the administrative heads under whom the committee functions.

...order signs for all necessary information...

C. Contacting all assistants two days prior to the meeting commitment. Some chairmen can be completely functional without supervision, others need reminders.
D. Writing letters of appreciation to all who participate in conducting the workshops.

Recommendations

The inservice training committee should sit in session once or twice a month during the school year. There will be a need for that many meetings and such meetings will give the members of the committee a feeling of camaraderie.

The committee should document the procedure and evaluate its effectiveness at least once a year.

The following time frame is practically standard and will allow for flexibility:

8:00 - 8:30	Registration
8:30 - 8:45	Announcements/Introductions
8:45 - 9:30	Morning Session
9:30 - 9:50	Coffee Break
9:50 - 11:30	Group participation or seminar activity
11:30 - 1:00	Lunch
1:00 - 3:00	Afternoon session
3:00 - 3:30	Closing Remarks and Dismissal

The appreciation of those trained and enriched by the activities of the committee will make the extra effort worthwhile and if conducted properly will develop into a recognized function of the school district.

chapter nine
responsibility of administrator

The secretary has a responsibility to the administrator but the administrator also has a responsibility to the secretary. For that reason I feel a few words to you as an administrator may be helpful to you both.

Working with someone — not for someone — is the key to career fulfillment. Self-motivated individuals work best in a cooperative atmosphere, and a self-motivated secretary who directs her initiative in constructive channels will be the kind of a secretary you want.

Following are some of the things to which you will need to direct your attention:

1. *Establish guidelines of authority* from the beginning of the boss-secretary relationship. Convey to her directly or indirectly just how far she can go in handling the affairs of your office. She can function more effectively if she knows just how much authority she has.
2. *Allow her to know your philosophy.* Discuss with your secretary the things you feel important to the job effort. There are opportunities to let her know "where you live" that will serve to help her realize her areas of authority. If she knows you well enough she can find her way, saving both of you from uncomfortable situations.
3. *Hold the reins.* Be candid about what you expect from her on the job. Be kind but firm. You are the boss and she expects you to be.
4. *Assign her meaningful work.* Nothing is so demoralizing as being given trivial work to do. Everything she does should fit into the overall picture whenever possible. There will be times, of course, when it will be necessary to ask her to perform menial tasks but if the office climate is good this will not matter.

5. *Encourage your secretary to be professional.* Provide opportunities for your secretary to grow on the job by furthering the inservice training efforts in your district. Let her know you appreciate everything she does to upgrade her skills. Encourage her to belong to her professional associations.
6. *Never tolerate office politics* if you are aware of them. Promote employees as a result of outstanding performance on the job or through recognized automatic progression. Those under you will lose respect for you if you promote from political pressure or "apple polishing."
7. *Be loyal to your secretary* and support her as you work with others. Remember her when the salary and personnel discussions take place. If you cannot support her, discuss the reasons why with her rather than with others around the office.

The life of a school administrator is difficult at best and it is important that you have an effective educational secretary by your side who can help to keep you secure in your role.

chapter ten
developing a "you"

This portion of *The Effective Educational Secretary* is written on a personal plane. I believe that success in life demands effort and those who are average must combine the talents we are given with a great deal of physical energy — get up and go!

The early years of our lives are usually so filled with growing physically and developing mentally that we seldom spend time in introspection.

Those of us who marry and rear families, as I did, spend our young adult lives concerned with the well-being of our families and have very little time for thinking about ourselves. There comes a time, however, in the lives of most of us when we begin to question ourselves in terms of our accomplishments, or lack of accomplishments. We review the things we've done and ponder on the things we wanted to do and haven't done. For this reason I've added the "Developing a 'You' " chapter to this book.

What is happiness? It's everything good! We seldom have all circumstances favorable enough to be completely happy, but we strive to have them nearly so. To me, a satisfactory life carries more meaning that a "happy" one completely free of cares and problems; however, solving our problems makes us better, more productive human beings and we need them to grow and blossom. It's important to learn to cope — to meet our troubles head-on instead of ducking them.

Each of us needs successful experiences to develop a good self-image and there are certain ways to lay the groundwork for such experiences. I've referred to some of them in previous sections of this book but they are important enough to bear repeating.

Be dignified.

I believe in preserving the dignity of every individual. Project an image of self-respect and be ever aware of the feelings of others. Never be guilty of tearing down another's self-respect!

Be gentle.

Gentleness is a softness of disposition and is one of the secrets of success in interacting with others. Gentleness is not an evidence of weakness; indeed, it is strength! Only the strong dare be gentle.

Be tolerant.

If it is not your nature to be tolerant of others, begin at once to try. One experience builds upon another until you gradually develop the tolerance so badly needed for your own peace of mind. Remember always that negative thoughts are more damaging to you than to others and tolerance of the actions of others is a positive experience.

Be understanding.

Empathy develops with experience — with "happenings." How many times have you said, "I know how you feel," and after weathering a similar experience realizing that your well-meaning words of comfort were really empty? Seeing other people as fellow human beings with the same feelings as you have builds empathy.

Being able to understand — to empathize — with others is a valuable safety valve for you. Bad temper is a destructive force and it's much easier to hold it in check if you are able to mentally "take the place of another." The saying that anger is one letter away from danger is true. Empathizing is a constructive force and one that contributes in a favorable way to your sound mental health.

Be generous.

Giving of yourself, whether it be time, energy, or worldly possessions is another of the good forces and reaps many rewards for most of us. Remember always that you're involved in developing *your* character and brightening *your* world and not trying to change others.

You can change your habits any time *you* feel the need to do so. Examine your heart. Are you generous? Do you think of ways to make life easier for others? You'll find after losing yourself in unselfish service to others some of your problems will have resolved themselves.

When you begin taking a look at yourself... refrain from being overly critical.

Be interested in others.

A genuine interest in others is a form of generosity and can lift you from a mundane existence to a fun world. Explore your relationship with those around you. Have you really taken time to question them, to search beyond the casual greeting? There is a world beyond yours that bears examination. It's not always easy to find something appealing in every individual but you can try! An honest effort makes a better person of you. You'll find to your surprise that your day will be filled with interesting anecdotes and experiences. People really are fun and have much to offer you if you approach them expectantly.

Be industrious.

From childhood we're taught that busy hands serve to keep us from boredom — a deadly state of mind. I believe this to be true. We tire from boredom — from lack of meaningful activity. We need periods of complete inactivity, of course, but I believe our bodies function more efficiently if we are physically active most of our waking hours.

Be mentally active, physically active and you'll be on your feet when others are falling around you. Don't be afraid of hard work! Be industrious and self-motivated.

Be constructively critical of self.

When you begin taking a look at yourself in terms of accomplishments, refrain from falling into the trap of being overly critical. Your self-esteem can be easily damaged and you'll lose your self-confidence. Many of us are our most severe critics. It's imperative to be honest, but there's danger in over analyzing. Treat yourself as you would others; be constructive when you criticize yourself. Be proud of your accomplishments and don't dwell on the things you've failed to do.

Be curious.

Don't be curious in a gossipy sense, but be eager to learn and know as much as you can about everything. You'll be in demand if you have a reservoir of information to share with others on appropriate occasions. Everything that is put together can somehow be taken apart and you need to be curious about the whole process. For every question there is some kind of answer. Ask questions and find the answers. It's a fun process.

Be open to new experience.

After you've entered the world of intellectual curiosity, don't fear to try something new. Although not everything new is good, you will find the perimeters of your world broadening as you test and "feel." You may be hurt at times but hurting is a necessary character building block. Experiment and grow.

Be resilient.

Work at quickly recovering your spirit — your good humor — when things do not go as you've planned. Bounce back twice as strong!

Be flexible.

You should be able to reverse your whole routine without ensuing panic. Organization is the key to a productive existence but few things are important enough that they can't be done another way. Learn to compromise as life is full of compromises. Just do the whole thing differently if needed.

Be good to look at.

Beauty can be facial as everything you are shows in your face. People are inclined to say that the beauty of soul is more than the beauty of feature, forgetting that the eyes and facial contours reflect our souls. Pinched features are never seen on anyone who can laugh and give lovingly of self.

Love yourself and love your fellow man in the broad sense of the word and let your face be a reflection of the good things you feel. You'll be effective as an educational secretary but most importantly, you'll be effective in the business of living!

part II

effectiveness principles at the educational site

Julia Maggs, Beverly Hills Unified School District, California

Sara Lomax, Wichita Public Schools, Kansas
Central Area Director of the National Association of Educational Office Personnel, 1986-87

Jean M. Faulkenberry, Fort Stockton Independent School District, Texas
President of the National Association of Educational Office Personnel, 1985-86

Ellen Dodd, Olympia School District, Washington

Carol M. Spencer, Davenport Public Schools, Iowa
President of the National Association of Educational Office Personnel, 1986-87

Sarah Clapp, Palm Springs Unified School District, California

Jackie Fuller, Boise State University, Idaho
Past President of the Idaho Association of Educational Office Personnel

chapter eleven
the effective
superintendent's secretary

By: Julia Maggs

    The expertise of the secretary to a school superintendent must incorporate all the skills mentioned in previous chapters with some very special additions.
    It is important to keep an "open door" to the superintendent's office at all times and not treat his/her office like a "castle with a moat around it." Whoever visits or calls the superintendent is a V.I.P. whether it be a staff member, a government official, a visitor to the city, a parent - especially a parent - and sometimes even a student. Occasionally the secretary can direct a visitor or phone call to another source without disturbing the superintendent but ninety-nine percent of the time this is not the case. If the secretary is aware the superintendent does not wish to be disturbed or is away from the office, then the appropriate thing to do is to set up an appointment and try to ascertain the subject matter or the problem so that the superintendent can be fully prepared with background information when the appointment comes around.
    It is known that a superintendent of schools is usually very active outside the district, being an attendee at most city council meetings; a participant on the board of directors and/or various committees of the local chamber of commerce; a member of the Rotary Club; and often the president or member of local or national business associations. Therefore, a plus for the secretary is to be able to immediately recognize voices on the phone of the superintendent's contacts/associates or their faces when visiting the office or attending a school function. This V.I.P. treatment by the secretary always has the effect of enhancing the boss' image - a secretary's goal at all times.

Good relations with staff members during school district coffee breaks, lunches, "after-hour" events, etc., are also a "must" for the superintendent's secretary. Always be ready to participate and willing to help in any way possible in the preparation of various activities held for birthdays, award presentation, retirements, holiday celebrations, etc. And most importantly, keep the superintendent informed of these upcoming occasions; mark the calendar; and if the superintendent cannot attend at any time, be there to offer apologies for the superintendent's absence and express congratulations, good luck wishes, etc. on the superintendent's behalf. Once again, you are attaining your goal of enhancing your boss' image.

The above and other situations will be handled very easily if the secretary possesses two very important qualities - patience with people and discretion on all subject matters. For example, there are many times when a parent will "storm" the superintendent's office unexpectedly demanding an audience right away. While waiting to see the superintendent, or alternatively setting up a date for a future appointment in his/her absence, the parent will want to expound on the "shabby treatment" his or her child is receiving by certain faculty members or other students; or even complain that the student is not being chosen for a certain athletic team or the annual school play. Despite a heavy load of work at this time, the secretary must be extremely patient and give the parent such time as he or she needs. Also, quite often residents will call to give the secretary a message for the superintendent outlining improvements which he or she considers ought to be made in the administration of the school district; in the discipline of the students; or the assignment of teachers. Here again, patience is needed to give due consideration to the caller.

It is in situations such as these that, in addition to the secretary displaying patience, the height of discretion must also be exercised. Other times discretion is needed are when the superintendent is visited by either a faculty member or student on a disciplinary matter, by a school board member, or by a resident or city official on a personal matter; and subsequent conversations can be overheard. To repeat any of the comments or opinions expressed at any time by student, teacher, parent or city official clearly would be breaking all confidentiality - a definite "no - no" for a superintendent's secretary.

Preparing for school board meetings and meeting other deadlines is a constant demand placed on a superintendent's secretary. Look for ways to improve the process and make suggestions to your superintendent. Insist on timely submissions of school board agenda items and back up material from the offices of the superintendent's subordinates, be sure to prepare a calendar of deadlines to be met after each school board meeting and give to your superintendent and appropriate subordinates.

Do all you can to help your superintendent to "keep out of trouble" and to "look good" in the eyes of school board members, the public, staff, and students.

Refer all inquiries from school board members to the superintendent, it is never right to reveal confidences of the superintendent to school board members or others. A superintendent must have complete trust and loyalty in his / her secretary for him / her to be an effective school superintendent.

It is now obvious that these are secretarial "extras" that will not only assist the superintendent in many ways but also make the secretary's duties more enjoyable and extremely worthwhile.

chapter twelve
the effective assistant superintendent's secretary

By: Sara Lomax, CEOE

Being an effective and efficient secretary to the assistant or deputy superintendent calls upon all of your resources, and then some more. Depending upon the size of the school district, the assistant superintendent generally is considered the hatchet man (or woman) that does all the dirty work while the superintendent creates a good public image. He has all the meetings, receives all the complaints the superintendent does not wish to handle, and does the disciplining in order for the superintendent to remain the "good guy." For these reasons, the assistant superintendent has to be a special person, and the secretary to the assistant superintendent must be an effective member of the team in order for the administrator to maintain physical and mental stamina.

Organization, Organization, and More Organization

Organization is important in any job, but in order to keep up with the demands of this office it is extremely important to be organized. An absolute *must* is a tickler file. A tickler file is merely an instrument to tickle your memory. A notebook binder kept at hand serves as the easiest form of a tickler file, indexed by month. This tickler should include all meetings, bulletins, and reports that are generally due and / or material to be prepared during that month.

Included in this would be a copy of the distribution list (Figure 1)

Figure 1

DISTRIBUTION LIST

Agenda and Minutes of All Administrators Meetings	320 copies - Distribution I - exclude NEA

Class Size Report (Do not send elementary to secondary and vice versa)	225 copies Elementary - Distribution I plus
	  2 copies - Local AFT
	  15 copies - Joint Class Size Committee
	  20 copies - Extras
	
	170 copies Jr. High - Distribution I plus
	  2 copies - Local AFT
	  15 copies - Joint Class Size Committee
	  20 copies - Extras
	
	140 copies Sr. High - Distribution I plus
	  2 copies - Local AFT
	  15 copies - Joint Class Size Committee
	  20 copies - Extras

Property Loss Entitlements	185 copies - Distribution III - include BOE
Administrators' Summer Vacation Schedule	255 copies - Distribution II

that indicates who will receive copies and how many copies are to be printed, plus any special people to receive the communication. A distribution code should be located in the front of the tickler notebook (Figure 2).

Figure 2

DISTRIBUTION CODE

Distribution I -	One for each principal, assistant principal, and secretary	270
	One for each division director	10
	Two for local NEA office	2
	One copy for each administrative building manager	15
	File copies	18
	Copies to be printed	315
Distribution II -	One copy for each principal	90
	One copy for each division director	10
	One copy for each coordinator and supervisor	140
	One copy for each BOE member	7
	File copies	13
	Copies to be printed	260
Distribution III -	Same as I, exclude secretaries, NEA, building managers	185

You may have as many distribution lists as deemed necessary.

Note that the school buildings' secretaries are included on some distribution lists. Their assistance is valuable to you, so make them feel like a part of the team. A rubber stamp saying "secretary" can be used to indicate their copies. This is helpful to them when it comes time to submit reports, update the school calendar, or just make sure the boss is at the right place at the right time.

A secondary tickler file consists of individual file folders in a file drawer close at hand for each day of the month. In these folders are placed agendas for meetings on that day, materials to be taken to the meetings, reminders to make a certain contact on that day, or reminders to your boss that a task is due the next week. A desk calendar cannot possibly hold all of the reminders you need, so do not trust your memory -- write it down! Each morning, remove contents to be used that day and place the agendas and meeting materials in a file folder marked "Materials For Today's Meetings" and place it on your administrator's desk.

Calendars

To get your boss to the right place at the right time, the calendar will be your most valued tool. If there was a fire in your office and you had time to take with you only what you could carry, other than your purse, the first thing you would probably grab would be the calendar. An assistant superintendent averages four to six scheduled meetings per day, depending on the size of the district, in addition to special meetings and separate appointments with individuals. Scheduling can become a headache for the secretary, especially when six to eight people with equally busy calendars are involved. A scheduling form is easy to develop. An example is found in Figure 3.

Figure 3

MEETING SCHEDULE FORM

MEETING SUBJECT: Textbook Rental Fees									LENGTH OF MEETING: 1 hr.	
DATE SET: April 10		TIME: 9:00-10:00				PLACE: Conference Room				
(Check dates below for availability of participants)										
NAME	MON. April 7		TUES. April 8		WED. April 9		THURS. April 10		FRI. April 11	CONFIRMED
	AM	PM	AM	PM	AM	PM	AM	PM	AM	PM	WITH
Jones	11:00-12:00	X	X	2:00-3:30	X	X	9:00-10:30 / 11:00-12:00	2:30-4:30	1:45-3:45	X	
H. Smith	OK			NO			OK NO	OK	OK		4/1 Carol
Black	NO			OK			OK OK	OK	OK		4/1 Doris
Green	NO			NO			OK NO	NO	NO		4/1 Mona
White	OK			OK			OK OK	OK	OK		4/1 Sue
Redd	OK			vac			OK OK	OK	NO		4/1 Pat

To use this form, remember your office probably has the busiest schedule so list four or five possible meeting times from your boss's calendar, then list the next busiest person, and so on down the line. Sometimes it is impossible to find a time compatible to all when scheduling a large group, so be sure to find out who must attend and who may attend if their calendar fits the time scheduled. Then start calling. After contacting a couple of offices the dates are soon narrowed down to just a few. Those on the lower end of the pecking order will have the fewest number of dates to consider! Then go back and confirm the meeting with each secretary. In the "confirmed" column, be sure to mark the date and person with whom the meeting time was confirmed. If time allows, it is always best to send a memo with information of the meeting. This is especially important if a meeting has been rescheduled.

You have a calendar on your desk and usually there is a calendar on the boss'desk. Train your boss not to schedule on the calendar without notifying you! At least once a week, compare the two calendars to make certain you have put all dates on your boss's calendar, and vice versa. This is a must if there is another secretary who might put a date on one calendar and not the other while you are away from your desk. Each afternoon, on a 3" x 5" card, type the next day's schedule with not only beginning and ending time and meeting location but also the subject of the meeting. Place this where your boss can pick it up each evening before leaving the office. This not only assists the administrator to know tomorrow's schedule in case an emergency should arise overnight, but assists his / her family to know the expected time of arrival the next evening.

Your calendar will deal not only with workday appointments, but also evening meetings, banquets, and programs. Your boss probably carries a pocket calendar. Ask for it at least once a month in order to put on evening events to which he / she is committed, as well as any business travel plans. Your administrator's spouse will appreciate this.

By January of each year, most professional organizations have published the dates of conferences and conventions for the coming school year. As soon as the school calendar is adopted you need to start scheduling meetings on next year's calendar. Set up a work calendar for each month on a 11" x 14" paper, marking in holidays, conventions, and other established meetings. Then start scheduling meetings for which your boss is responsible. The only office it is essential to check for conflicts is the superintendent's, or if there is more than one assistant superintendent check also with their scheduling secretaries. If there are multiple assistant superintendents, there is usually a pecking order. As soon as your calendar is set, including meeting room reservation, make copies of it for the secretaries of other assistant superintendents or directors who are responsible for setting meetings so they can schedule their calendar.

By April, send bulletins to members of each committee your boss chairs, listing the dates and times of meetings for next year. Send a second copy to the recipient's secretary and ask that the dates be immediately put on the calendar. There may be some movement of positions in the district, but at least the calendar has been set so members can schedule around the meetings. In a loose leaf binder, set up a divider for each committee and place the bulletin that lists meetings for the year in the proper section. In each section, have a list of all the members of that committee and the number of copies to be printed when distributing materials to the committee. It does not hurt to send the bulletin a second time (with the current date) in August in case there is a change of personnel or the secretary did not get the dates recorded.

Many districts have a master calendar on which all meetings and activities are listed for the year, including professional and employee organizations. It is usually distributed to all schools, offices, and organization leaders at the beginning of the school year. A copy of the master calendar reproduced in the monthly district newsletter is helpful to all employees.

Telephone and Office Communications

How you communicate with others on the phone or in the office is extremely important in your position. While you have been doing all of the above scheduling on the telephone, did you ever think of how you came across to the party at the other end? Were you considerate of their problems? Did you try not to convey a one-upsmanship?

Get to know each of the other secretaries with whom you frequently communicate. Go out to lunch occasionally and get to know them and any peculiarities of their offices. In one district, all cabinet level secretaries try to meet for lunch every other month. If a certain problem has arisen, it is talked out and everyone leaves feeling good. It is also a social time where you get to know the voices on the other end of the line.

Visitors to your office expect a "high class" secretary, so do not let them down. Be friendly, appropriately dressed, and professional. Should the visitor have to wait, offer a cup of coffee or maybe just some friendly conversation, which might include asking if they are from your city, or if not how long they have been there and where they are from. People love to talk about themselves and the weather. If the visitor is an irate patron, such conversation and pleasantries will soften the patron for your boss. Don't share a point of view with the irate visitor -- just assure them you understand their concern.

You will probably have some contact with the media. When they call to speak to your boss, try to ascertain the subject of the call so you can have information available for your boss when he/she speaks to them. Familiarize yourself with which reporter covers which beat. Never tell tales out of school to anyone!

When speaking with someone, either on the phone or in person, be sure you get the name. Nothing is more sacred to a person than their name, and when talking with them be sure to refer to them by name. In that manner, they will know you have been paying attention to them. Make it a point never to pick up the phone unless you have pencil and paper at hand and are prepared to jot down the name of the person and other pertinent information at the very beginning of the conversation.

Know ahead of time who should be put through to your boss regardless of who is with him/her. Unless it is an extreme emergency, do not interrupt your boss. Politely inform the caller that the administrator is in a meeting that is scheduled to be out at a certain time. If it looks like the boss will not be able to return the call until a later time, tell the caller when to expect the call, and try to find out the purpose of the call. If your boss has not returned the call by that time, call the person and say that your administrator is unable to return the call until a certain time. If you know the subject, ask if you may transfer the call to another administrator who you *know* to be in. If you don't know the subject, politely ask what the call is about so you can refer the call if necessary. Keep all telephone messages on your desk so you can keep track of who has been called.

Get the messages to your boss as soon as possible. If there is a chance you will not be at your desk when your boss is on the way out of the office, have a designated place for these messages so he / she can determine the need to return the call. There may be a call that is important and an early return call will eliminate work, bad feelings, or other equally unpleasant happenings. If your boss enjoys placing calls, work out a system so you will know whose calls have been returned.

Protocol

Today many more administrators are receiving PhD or EdD degrees. Granted, they have worked hard to receive the degree and want everyone to know they have it, but there is protocol involved which shows this respect. When addressing a person with a doctoral degree, either written or verbal, use the title before the name. Do not use the title before the name of the person sending the communication. This is construed as one-upsmanship. For example, a memo would be addressed:

To: Dr. John W. Smith, Principal

From: Robert S. Jones, Deputy Superintendent

or the closing salutation of a letter could read:

> Robert S. Jones, PhD
> Deputy Superintendent

Many administrators prefer not to have the initials following the name. When placing a call for your administrator, say "Robert Jones is calling for Dr. Smith."

If a memo is addressed to more than one person, list them in rank order. The same applies to the listing of those whom you have copied at the end of a letter or memo. If all recipients are of the same level, then list them in alphabetical order.

When arranging seating at banquets or places in reception lines a similar procedure is followed. The higher the rank, the closer to the podium or front of the receiving line. If you are responsible for seating arrangements at Board of Education meetings, a pecking order is usually used. In most districts, the vice president sits next to the president, and then those with the greatest number of years of service are closest to the president. When more than one new member is elected, they are seated according to the number of votes received. In other districts, the Board president directs the seating of members in whatever manner he / she chooses. Find out before you need it the correct procedure used in your district or what your boss wishes done in these and other similar situations.

Confidentiality

Confidentiality is a *must* in your job. You will see things going across your desk, and your boss will tell you things that must not be spoken about with others outside the office. Respect the confidence the boss has in you by not repeating confidential information. Mail marked "confidential" means it is something that is not to be opened by just anyone or left lying around on a desk for anyone to see. "Privileged" means to be opened only in your office, not by the mail room. "Personal" means for the eyes of the addressee only.

Filing

Nothing is more frustrating than for your administrator to ask for a certain piece of correspondence and not be able to find it. Organize your files. A very good reference is *File It Right and Find It,* a records management manual prepared especially for use in the educational office. Have a reference sheet at the front of your files listing all of the categories in your files and what is placed in each category. It is also advisable to have an alphabetized cross reference guide.

If the boss has the habit of stacking mail on his / her desk to be taken care of later, find out the system of what is in each stack, and maybe even offer suggestions of how it might be improved, such as file folders or desk trays labeled Immediate Action, Action Needed, a specific topic Reference, Reply Needed, Routine Bulletins (from other offices), Publications (newsletters, periodicals, house organs, etc.). When sorting the mail, use folders for each day of the week with topics such as: Monday's Correspondence; Monday's Mail, Immediate Action Required; Monday's Mail, Action Needed; Monday's Mail, Approval Needed. This is especially helpful if your boss tends to leave mail in the folder for a couple of days and is not sure what he / she has or has not read. Make copies of agendas, materials for upcoming meetings, or reports due before placing on your administrator's desk. Place them in the appropriate folder tickler file. Notes tend to get lost on a desk, so have a designated location or holder on the administrator's desk or your desk for special messages.

Accuracy and Neatness

Secretaries in other offices tend to look to you and the superintendent's secretary as an example of the professional secretary. Do not let them down. Be not only neat in your appearance, but neat in your work and your work environment. Proof all work carefully. As the saying goes, errors never appear on a page until after it has been printed! If there is more than one secretary in your office, get into the habit of having one of them proof your work and you should be available to proof theirs. This not only helps the image of your office, but allows the other secretaries to know what is going on. One school district is in the process of having all office employees take a course in the art of proofreading, and after they are trained, each subsequent new office employee will be given the course. Some districts offer business inservice courses for office employees during work hours.This enables all employees to improve themselves and not have to worry about attending classes on their own time and with their own money.

In all probability, you were hired, among other things, because of your proven skills. And because of that, whether it is true or not, you must take it upon yourself to catch any spelling or grammatical errors your boss might make and correct them. Just because your boss said or wrote the errors does not make them right. Do not be afraid to correct them. Your boss will appreciate your help. Some bosses give their secretaries free reign in correcting the composition of correspondence,others are a little more possessive of their authorship. Just make sure *you* are correct when you do the changing! There are many excellent reference books to keep at your desk for just such a purpose. A spelling dictionary, a reference manual for secretaries, and, of course, an updated dictionary are musts for any secretary's desk.[2]

Do not allow work to stack up on your desk. Use in and out baskets to keep your desk neat. Keep frequently used material in notebooks to eliminate desk clutter.

Hints to Eliminate Unnecessary Work

Most all school districts have become automated in some manner. Personal computers are taking the place of typewriters in some district offices. Sophisticated word processing terminals connected to the main frame and memory typewriters are the rule rather than the exception in today's educational office. Use them. Don't be afraid of progress. They are put there to make your work easier. Note the word "easier" and not "reduce your work load." They will make your work easier and faster and will allow you to do work that you did not have time for previously. Typing all of those form letters is now a snap with the use of automation. A letter that is personalized and typewritten does much more for the public relations image of your district than the old xerox copy addressed to a general group.

Lables are a must. How many times have you spent time addressing envelopes when you should have been doing something else? Most all data processing equipment runs labels from the personnel and pupil data base. Do not think that is something only to be used in personnel and school offices--you use them, also. Order labels to your specification, or if your personal computer or word processor has the capabilities to run labels, avail yourself of that procedure. Have a set of labels for every type of mailing you need and keep several copies of each set on hand so you can use them at a moment's notice. Have sets for board of education members, state legislators (both for home and office), for each distribution list referred to before, all administrators and supervisors, members of all committees that you are responsible for sending agendas and minutes, vendors, and so on.

Miscellaneous Tips

Be a professional secretary by joining your local, state, and national associations for educational office personnel.[3] These organizations offer certification programs for personal and professional development of their members, as well as professional growth publications. Do not be just a joiner, be a participant. A personnel director once wrote that when interviewing potential employees she always looked at what community and professional organization the applicant belonged to and how actively involved. She said this was one measure of a person's ability to work with others and their desire to learn.

Whenever inservice training or workshops are offered in the area of your profession, by all means sign up! You may have had courses in school in business English or communications, but styles change constantly and you are never too old to learn. If your district offers continuing education classes in business classes or computers, sign up! Even if you do not currently have a computer, you will probably have one in the not too distant future. Not only that, you will be able to "speak the language" with those that do. If you do not have access to continuing education classes or a college or university in your locale, take advantage of correspondence courses.[4] I was once asked by my daughter as to when I would stop going to class. My reply: When they stop having them.

Learn all you can about your district and the total education program. Don't just glance at reports and brochures that cross your desk, read them. Absorb all that you can about your district. Learn the names of all administrators, and try to be able to identify them on sight and speak to them by name. Know the location of each school and administrative building in your district. If your district allows visitation time, visit as many other offices and school offices as possible. Get to know their physical environment. There may come a time that you need to contact someone but the telephone is continually busy. If you know whose office is close by, you can contact that office to get a message through. After visiting some school offices you may have a little more empathy for the school secretary. One district has an inservice day for all non certificated employees who have passed their probationary period. This day is spent touring selected administrative buildings, schools at each level, and plant maintenance facilities. These employees have a feeling of belonging after these tours, and have expressed appreciation for being allowed the time to see the functions of each area of the district.

Rewards

Being secretary to an assistant or deputy superintendent has its rewards. Prestige is only one very small part of it. The variety and the challenges of the tasks of this office are the ingredients for an interesting job. When administrators advance to the position of deputy or assistant superintendent they have to be a special type of person. You know they are experts in their chosen field and naturally they are well educated, but they are also something else. Generally, they are chosen because their expertise is just a bit broader, their leadership ability is superior, their ability to communicate with others is outstanding, and their understanding of people puts them a step above the rest. For those reasons, you are working with a unique person who makes it easy to do your job -- so do it well, and enjoy!

References

1. *File It Right and Find It,* National Association of Educational Office Personnel, 1902 Association Drive, Reston, VA 22091 - 1502

2. *Instant Spelling Dictionary,* (latest edition), Career Institute, 555 East Lange St., Mundelein, IL 60060

    The Gregg Reference Manual, (latest edition), McGraw-Hill Book Company, New York

3. For more information about organizations in your area, write to the National Association of Educational Office Personnel, 1902 Association Drive, Reston, VA 22091 - 1502.

4. A correspondence course designed specifically for educational office employees, with a Business Administration Certificate issued upon completion, is offered by The Pennsylvania State University, Department of Independent Learning, 128 Mitchell Building, University Park, PA 16802.

chapter thirteen
the effective high school secretary

By: Jean M. Faulkenberry CEOE

" Effective " is defined as producing a decided, decisive, or desired effect. Effective emphasizes the actual production of, or the power to produce an effect; may suggest an acting or a potential for action or use in such a way as to avoid loss or waste of energy in effecting, producing, or functioning.

A "high school" is an institution for educating young people and is usually composed of grades nine through twelve although many variations of grade combinations may be on a given campus; i.e., only one grade, two or three grades, or all grades. High school offices are varied in over-all structure from campus to campus. Staffing is influenced by student population, curriculum offerings, and by budget.

"Secretary" is defined as a confidential employee employed to handle correspondence and manage routine detail work.

Now, look at the "effective high school secretary" as a highly-skilled, thoroughly-trained, self-motivated office professional working in a unique situation. The title actually may be secretary, or it might be clerk, bookkeeper, data processor, executive secretary, administrative assistant, or some other. The intent of this chapter is not to define a job description but to recognize the responsibilities of the high school office staff.

In a small school, the office may have only one secretary who does it all; in larger schools, there will be multistaffing successfully handling the duties of receptionist, telephone operator, mail processor, accountant, nurse, cashier, records retention manager, payroll clerk, insurance specialist, pupil attendance clerk, or key operator. The office staff will also maintain staff records, obtain substitute teachers, post grades, forward student transcripts, figure class ranks, make graduation arrangements, control inventories, serve as purchasing agents, supervise student aides, manage the office, do minor machine maintenance, schedule activities, maintain the master calendar, and serve as activity sponsor. This list is not meant to be comlete because the bottomline is that the effective high school secretary is a member of the educational team that educates youth by direct or indirect student contact. The primary role is to provide support where needed.

Qualifications for the position will be determined by the school and the profile of the employee might be: age, just out-of-school to past-normal-retirement; education, on-the-job training to a masters degree; family status, single to grandparent; sex, male or female; experience, none to much. The necessary skills for effectiveness can be divided into three categories: people skills, survival skills and technical skills. No attempt is made to declare which skill is the most important because they are "a package deal." All are essential elements for educational office personnel effectiveness not only for high schools but for all levels.

People Skills

People skills are communication skills and are at the very core of effectiveness. Problems result from communication breakdown and then misunderstandings arise. Good communication skills promote positive public relations. The effective high school secretary will promptly and courteously greet persons - all persons - who enter the office, make them feel at ease and important. The secretary will screen visitors, and escort or direct them to their destination. Proper introductions will be made. The secretary remains calm and courteous when handling difficult visitors, extending the same cordial reception as extended the more pleasant visitor.
The telephone is answered promptly and correctly. When calls must be transferred, an explanation is given. Wrong numbers are greeted with the same pleasant voice as correct numbers. Messages are taken correctly and promptly delivered. Outgoing calls

are handled as per requested, and information about available telephone services is kept handy. Personal calls are non-existent to very limited.

The high school secretary compiles information to compose written communications from letters to reports to memoranda. Written communications are edited using writing-spelling-grammar-sentence structure skills, and demonstrates initiative in composing responses to routine correspondence. Information for specific purposes is organized and analyzed.

Some type of fast note-taking is essential and transcription is flawless. Typing is swift and accurate with special attention to the over-all appearance.

Records are kept up-to-date, filed promptly and retrieved instantly. The "File It Right and Find It" system was developed by the National Association of Educational Office Personnel (NAEOP) specifically for educational offices. The book is available from NAEOP, 1902 Association Drive, Reston, VA 22091.

A reference library consisting of a dictionary, telephone directory, zip code directory, resource materials, desk manual, and school policies is kept at hand and used.

A professional attitude is always maintained. Flexibility and adaptability allows working well under pressure, conducting oneself in a courteous, business-like manner. Tact is always used.

Body language is carefully monitored as actions speak as loudly as words. No difference is made between receiving a defiant student, an upset teacher, an irate parent, the superintendent of schools or the president of the school board. EVERYBODY IS SOMEBODY and is entitled to be treated with respect and courtesy. The effective high school secretary takes the initative in being helpful.

Survival Skills

Survival skills allows handling stress, establishing a smooth workflow that produces positive results. A good self-image is of utmost importance. One who does not feel good about oneself cannot feel good toward others. A close self-examination will provide direction as to where improvement is needed.

Confidence is the key to a positive self-image and can be developed through many self-initiated activities. Continuing education will provide reinforcement and is available through many sources at little or no cost. Workshops, inservices, and institutes provided by educational professional organizations are excellent. The NAEOP provides this at the national level and is the only national association specifically for educational office personnel. Most states in the United States have state-level organizations. If this information is not elsewhere available, NAEOP can provide it. Local and/or area organizations are encouraged. Assistance will be provided in organizing and strengthening groups of educational office personnel to provide their own professional growth. NAEOP has also developed the Professional Standard Program (PSP) of personal professional growth and certification. Information is available from NAEOP, 1902 Association Dr., Reston, VA 22091.

Community colleges, universities, adult education units, school district sponsored seminars and community involvement are other sources of professional growth opportunities. Take advantage of the workshops sponsored by equipment manufacturers. The more knowledgeable one is the more confidence one has.

Physical soundness supports a positive self-image. Careful attention should be given to basic nutrition, a schedule which includes adequate rest and relaxation, and a sensible exercise program makes both body and mind function better. As important as companionship is, some time must be reserved just for self.

A person who feels attractive is attractive. Careful attention should be given to grooming and dress should be appropriate. Do not wait to be told what the proper dress is; observing the overall atmosphere of the office and the other people in it will make "the proper" very obvious. The office is no place for fads. Be conservative and neat.

Promptness is of top priority. Nothing makes a day fall apart quicker than to arrive at a busy office late. Arrangements must be made to arrive a little early so as to have time to "get organized" and not have to "regroup." A high school office seldom runs as "per schedule" due to the large number of people involved, the emergencies that must be taken care of, the unexpected events, the people who suddenly appear without appointments but with needs to be met immediately, the bus that arrives late, and the list could go on and on. Interruptions are a way of life in a high school office.

The high school secretary is "always there" It seems that all other persons have acceptable reasons to be absent once in a while, but the secretary is expected to be on the job every day . . . and night . . . week-end . . . and holidays.

Take care of over-all health. Regular physical checkups are a must. Disposition is influenced by the way a person feels physically and the high school office is no place for a sour face. A good sense of humor is a must.

Technical Skills

Knowledge is the most important of all the technical skills and essential knowledge for the effective high school secretary covers many areas.

It is understood that a high school secretary has the necessary job skills such as typing, ten-key adding machine, computer literacy and operator training, note-taking, filing, etc. The high school secretary will know the other equipment such as copying machines and will be able to make minor repairs or at least know when to call the service company.

A knowledge of the community should be a top priority. Know the culture, the history, the geography, the living standard, the economy and the moral climate of the community. Be able and willing to accept people for what they are rather than what a single standard might dictate. Be able to give directions to any place within the community as there will be parents, students, salesmen and servicemen new to the area who come into the high school office.

Loyalty is second nature to the effective high school secretary. Express pride in the school, the community, the state, the nation and "the system." Show confidence in your administrators.

A thorough understanding of the school district is necessary. The general philosophy, the district policies, the campus rules, personnel and their responsibilities, budget implications, organizational structure, staffing, state statutes, and the legislative process are just a few things that must be learned.

Complete specific details as to the job one is expected to perform, and the means to accomplish the desired results are necessities. Determine through open communication how each portion of the overall operation affects the other parts. Understand the authority, the restrictions, and the limitations of each area of job assignment.

Be knowledgeable of inventories, supplies, personnel, shopping practices and storage facilities. Keep up with new products and be prepared to make recommendations for improvements in equipment and services.

Know and follow the chain of command. Recognize confidentiality and ethical responsibilities. Use logic in problem solving and decision making.

Be willing to accept change. If skills get rusty, put in a little extra time studying, practicing, or learning to operate a new piece of equipment. Do not hesitate to ask for help, direction or assistance.

Managing time more effectively in order to develop professional skills and complete job duties concurrently when a strict schedule is not enforceable is a real challenge, and is one of the most wide-spread problems of high school secretaries. This brief exercise is included to assist in time management and also stress control.

Analyze time management techniques by answering honestly, on paper, these questions:
... What are the five most significant things, situations, and people that waste my time at work?
... How have I dealt with each of the five things in the past?
... What seemed to work in controlling these time wasters?
... What could I have done to deal more effectively with those things and people that wasted my time?
... When did I really have a handle on my time this week?

Review the answers alone and then with another person who is familiar with how you use your time. After the review, answer the following questions (on paper):
... How can I, on my own, improve my time management skills?
... How do I waste my time at work?
... How do I waste others' time at work?
... What are my short-term goals related to time management?
... What can I do to realize these goals?

Over the next two weeks, I will do the following to help myself realize these goals:

... Step 1

... Step 2

... Step 3

The more effective the high school secretary is in eliminating time wasters and managing daily activities the more time will be available to devote to self-improvement. Time should be a benefactor, not a distractor. Effective time management provides stress control and enhances job effectiveness.

In conclusion, the most important statement of the chapter on "The Effective High School Secretary" is to remember that everything that is said and done has an influence on someone. The attitude with which it is said or done determines if the reception is positive or negative. The high school secretary can either be a positive or a negative influence in the life of someone else. Only the secretary can make that choice.

chapter fourteen
the effective middle school secretary

By: Ellen Dodd

By the time I had finished my first day as a middle school secretary, I was really beginning to question my sanity. I had waited a long time for an opening and was excited when the call finally came explaining that there was an opening at the middle school across town. I can remember that morning well----driving across town, parking my car, straightening my dress and hoping to make a good impression, walking into the office, expecting..... well, I guess I didn't know what to expect. I barely had time to put down my purse. The telephones were ringing, the teachers were in and out of the office getting ready for classes to start, the principals were getting the day's appointments and meetings in order and KIDS EVERYWHERE!!!! Kids needing lunch tickets, needing to call home for necessities forgotten, needing lockers opened and extra pencils and everyone asking what seemed to me endless questions to which I had no answers. Finally the bell rang and before long, the halls and the office were quiet. I knew that I was a good secretary, but I had never felt so inadequate in all my life!! I went home that day very discouraged and wondered if this job was really meant for me. Only time and experience would show me how very rewarding and gratifying this crazy job really was.

Qualifications for a middle school secretary are varied. In my opinion, good organizational skills are number one---for without them, even the best secretary would certainly get lost in the shuffle of a busy school office. You will begin to develop skills in organizing your time and motion as each situation dictates. I have found that one of the easiest methods of keeping track of oral instructions and "things to do" is to keep a steno pad on your desk and within easy reach at all times, ready to take notes and directions. Date each page and if time permits, even note the hour of the day. This sometimes proves to be helpful later when verifying the exact time a telephone conversation took place or a package was delivered and might make a big difference if a question might arise later. By jotting down instructions of who to call, a change in a child's address, a letter to write, or a paragraph to change in a previous letter, these "things to do" can not only be crossed off when accomplished, but can be referred to in the following weeks. I could always thumb back through my pages and come up with an answer to even the smallest of details. When you have finished a task and have crossed it off your list, it is helpful to jot down any additional information you feel to be pertinent or that could possibly answer a question later on. Getting a person's full name at the conclusion of a telephone conversation could save precious time in the future if additional information was needed. For future reference, you might note the proper person to contact for a particular need or an address that might need to be corrected. Whatever the case, this information might come in handy for later use.

Keeping a set of file folders within easy reach is also helpful in keeping your office running smoothly. "Things To Do," "Reports Due," Information Only," and "Filing" folders help keep stray papers from getting misplaced on your desk and in the office. Along with these folders, other folders can be used to collect requested forms, data, classlists and other important information requested from teachers, form letters, information for monthly reports, and any other information that you rely on often and need at your fingertips.

A dictionary and a good secretarial reference book are also necessities on a school secretary's desk. In composing, drafting and typing correspondence of any kind, the point is to get the message across clearly, concisely, and in a friendly but business-like manner. Having reliable office reference material at your disposal is of great assistance in word usage, punctuation, spelling and correct office letter formats, and is also a great time saver----and with the constant interruptions in a school office, this is a must!

Keep an appointment calendar, either the desk size or a desk-blotter size. This will help organize the day, hour by hour. Use this to note both the administrator's activities and your own---including doctor appointments, vacation days, meetings, special seminars or any time that either of you will be out of the office. Noting in advance the days when you will have substitutes in your school (i.e. for seminars, workshops, or instruction days) will help you to prepare forms, keys, payroll cards, and instructions and will help alleviate any last minute confusion in getting your substitutes signed in, and sent on their way with all the necessary questions answered in advance. You might keep a wall calendar also and use this to note the entire school's commitments. This can be quite helpful in checking the school's appointments and meetings a day, month, quarter or semester at a glance. This calendar could be used to chart special events such as "Back To School Night," the Halloween Carnival, the annual Christmas Pagent, Parent Conferences, Winter Recess, Spring Break, and all school holidays as well as dates your school might schedule for community use. Local scout troups and church groups using your facilities might also be noted in order to avoid duplication in scheduling.

Along with good secretarial and organizational skills, there are certain qualifications for a good middle school secretary that are rarely included on a resume. I hardly know where to begin, for these inner-qualities flow naturally together and are so basic, not only in dealing with 10-14 year olds in a middle school setting, but in dealing and working with other adults on a day-to-day basis. Be polite, be courteous, be cheerful, but the most important is to have a good positive attitude. Setting about your daily duties with a "whistle-while-you-work" attitude make the day go much more smoothly and makes the office a pleasant and more productive place to be. Teachers, administrators, and parents alike will enjoy coming into your office. The secretary and the office are the "hub" of the school and generally her attitude is carried out throughout the school. If she is a grumbler and a complainer, the staff and parents will avoid her and may only come to her out of sheer necessity or may side-step her judgment completely, by going over her head to the school administrator with the most trivial of problems. This not only is an example of an unfriendly and unproductive office climate, but is a waste of the administrator's time, when the problem could easily have been solved by a helpful and competent secretary.

You will need to rely on your good sense of humor in order to survive the constant flow of "priority problems" and the unending interruptions. Children of all ages (even the grown-up kind) are sure that *their* particular problem needs to be handled at that precise moment and should be number one on *your list* of "things to do." Being angry about how over-worked you are and how little you are appreciated will not help solve their problem or yours! Handle each problem as it arises as best you can, and if the solution to their problem is not readily available, or is something you cannot answer, let them know that you'll be checking it out for them; then if you cannot find the answer, find someone who can! (This is a prime example of using your steno pad to jot down the problem. Then when time allows, refresh your memory and get the problem solved or the question answered.)

Flexibility is the key to your mental survival, for without this personal trait, most middle school secretaries would be out the door before the end of the first day! Plans may change at the drop of a hat and that means you have to stop.....take a deep breath.... and then forge ahead. Learn to bounce back when things do not go as you had planned. It might be a shortage of paper needed for a special project, or a deadline that was forgotten until the last minute; maybe a report that has to be retyped at the end of a busy day. Being flexible means being able to cope with a change in a situation easily, being open minded, being able to compromise, and having the ability to look disappointment in the eye and still smile, smile, smile!!! It is the ability to face your daily tasks with the added edge of a positive attitude that makes the work a challenge and the school climate enjoyable.

Now comes the challenging part of being a middle school secretary. A school secretary wears many hats and needs to offer a variety of talents. She needs to be not only a terrific secretary, organized in every facet, but also a loving mother, a gentle nurse, a warm friend and a counselor who is willing to stop...and listen to some often heart-wrenching tale from kids who are at a mixed-up time in their lives. These qualities, which fall on the emotional side, are equally as important in a good school secretary as typing or shorthand skills. Why? Because this job differs from any other secretarial position in one key factor----the kids!! They are what makes this job so special. They keep us on our toes and keep us young at heart, and by reaching out to them, and giving of ourselves, we truly are the ones who benefit.

Being able to deal with people is another must-----for without effective communication, a school office is chaos. Communication is the key word in all aspects, but especially between administrator and secretary. The principal sets the mood with the office and it is the secretary's duty to portray that image through careful composing and construction of all bulletins, memos and correspondence. The secretary who can construct concise and accurate sentences, will have a better sense of control over the office when she knows that her written communications are clear and to the point. Because of her accuracy in getting the message across, fewer mistakes will be made, and thus less time spent by the secretary. If a memo is sent out and the questions are not worded clearly, the office might receive incorrect information, have to rewrite the memo, and then wait again for the responses to come in. Expressing yourself clearly the first time will save you time in the long run.

Good telephone communication skills are also at the top of the list of importance. When you answer the telephone, have a smile in your voice. Remember, you are representing your school to the person on the other end of the line. Be sure to identify yourself and your school. Politely ask who is calling and what you might do to help them--this helps tremendously in relaying the message to your principal and in supplying him / her with essential files and other needed materials to aid in answering questions. If the caller is angry----listen. Let them vent their anger. After listening to their problem, let them know how their problem can be handled, either by referring them to your administrator or by handling the problem yourself. Do not take their anger personally. They are angry at the situation, not at you. Always take the caller's name and the number where they can be reached and verify this information by repeating the information. Reading back this information greatly reduces errors.

Be sure you understand how to use your telephone properly. Use the "hold" button when the caller cannot immediately be connected to the proper party. Be polite and let the caller know you are putting them on hold. Check back with your caller to keep them posted on the situation. "I'm sorry, Mr. Kelly's line is still busy. Would you like to hold or shall I take a message?" Always answer your phone promptly. Transferring calls accurately is also very important. You can do this by informing the caller that he needs to be connected with another party, and that you would be glad to transfer his call for him. You might say "Hold on please, I am transferring your call now." Common courtesy is the key word in telephone etiquette.

Accurate and legible message taking is a must in a busy school office. Be sure to listen carefully and if something is not clear, have the caller repeat the message. Ask for proper spelling of names and companies. Repeating the information to the caller insures proper messages and verifies that the information was taken correctly. Deliver all messages promptly.

Setting up a tickler file is an easy way to keep track of daily, weekly, and monthly duties and will remind you of important follow-up dates. This file should be organized by the days of the month, with dividers for each month of the year. A 3"x5" card file works nicely and can sit right on your desk within easy reach. File your reminder cards behind the day you should start working on that particular project and you're all set to go. Note any information necessary in accomplishing your task, being sure to list the date the project, letter, or report is due. These reminders are life-savers and help to better organize your routine, day by day and month by month.

It is important that you be discreet in working with student files and confidential information regarding your staff. Cumulative files follow students throughout their school life and may contain certain material meant to be kept private. Along the same lines, employee files are only for your administrator's access and the knowledge you possess must be kept to yourself. If this trust between administrator and secretary is broken by revealing confidential information or parts of private conversations, then a large aspect of your professionalism has been lost. Avoid office gossip and politics altogether.

Last, but by no means least, be able to sort through your

work each day and set work priorities for the following day's workload. Give yourself 20 minutes at the end of the day to look through your "in-basket" and across your desk top for things needing to be completed in the early part of the next day. Sort these jobs into a stack with the high priority items on the top. Making a list of "things to do" for the next day can also help you to "keep on track" and get high priority jobs done on time. Flipping ahead in your calendar and making a notation of special reports due and follow-up work to be done can prevent rushing through a job to meet a deadline. Keeping your desk and work area organized and efficiently run will save countless hours in wasted time and mismanaged motion.

In closing, a middle school is a very special place to work. It is a place of principals and vice principals doing their best to create a stimulating curriculum to enrich the intellect of these 10-14 year olds who, at this phase in their development, are neither children nor adults, but are young people "in the middle." The middle school is a place of teachers striving to enlighten young minds and to stretch the thinking process to new found heights. And it lastly is a place for a school secretary who is rewarded daily by the love and affection of a group of kids "in the middle."

chapter fifteen
the effective elementary school secretary

By: Carol M. Spencer, CEOE, CPS

Elementary school secretaries are unique! Dependent upon the district; we sometimes have to: play nurse, sell lunch tickets and milk, babysit, discipline, handle an all-school moneymaker, handle lunch applications, attendance, supplies, resale, service books, enrollment reports, book inventory, student records, immunization records, payrolls, grade reporting, state and federal reports, requisitions, be a receptionist, handle all phone calls, etc., etc., etc.

In some schools we have part time aides to help, part time nurses and even some half time principals (they share two buildings.)

An elementary school secretary generally arrives at least one half hour to forty-five minutes early, because she knows that will be her last quiet time for the rest of the day. At this time of the day she prepares the office. She will have a list of the things she would like to accomplish by the end of the day, i.e., finish enrollment report, balance out service fees, send folders to another school for several students who have just moved, etc.

The phone rings several times, parents calling in to let the school know about their student's absence. The elementary school secretary writes them down on a call-in sheet on the counter. The sheet is divided by alphabetical squares. Later when the attendance is sent down from the individual rooms, she will enter the absent students on the sheet also. She marks "CI" in front of the names of students whose parents have called-in.

A half-time teacher-in-charge will call the parents of those who have not called in and find out the reason for their student's absence. The names are then posted to computer sheets by an aide in the office assigned thirty minutes a day for that particular assignment.

Meanwhile back at the counter---the teachers start arriving for the day, picking up their keys and checking in. Some have questions, some smile and say hello, some mumble and head for their rooms, again depending on the day of the week, time of the year or even dependent upon the way the wind is blowing. If it is raining, it is a definite mumble.

The central office substitute caller calls and tells the secretary she will have two substitutes today and who they will be replacing. She pulls two sub-sheets from the drawer and places them on the counter in preparation for their arrival.

Two students come in from the playground, one for his morning medication, the other with a bloody nose. The secretary gives the bloody nose a wet paper towel, the other student his medication. (The school secretary has taken a course on medical procedures and has been approved and certified.) She finds the principal and tells him who the other half of the bloody nose is and he says he will take care of the problem when the kids come in from the playground.

More phone calls, medications, skinned knees, subs, teachers and the bell rings for the students to come in to the building---- THE DAY OFFICIALLY BEGINS!!

The secretary then greets the children who were unable to make it to class on time and issues a late slip and marks it on the official attendance sheet. The part time aide in the office come in and starts on the attendance. The other part time aide comes in and helps with several students in the nurse's office. Later she helps with the resale, counting items out for placement in the teachers boxes, etc., etc., etc.

Several new students walk in the door with their parents, one without. She gives them enrollment forms, immunization and free lunch forms to fill out. The reading specialist is called to the office for placement of the students.

We try and contact the parents of the students who came without the parent. No luck. No phone. The child has a blue transfer card from another school in our district in her hand, and knows her address, which is in our district. We send the appropriate forms with her and place her in a class. She returns them the next day.

Our half time teacher-in-charge notices that one of our students has been absent for several days without a call-in and she has not been able to contact the parents because there is not a phone in the home. She contacts our Truant Officer, she heads out the door for her class and says the Truant Officer will be in contact with the secretary, would she please take care of the message.

Payrolls are due the next day and the secretary takes out the computer forms from the central office payroll department. She gathers up the absence slips of the teachers who have been out and matches them up to the daily cards she keeps with the name of the person who has been absent, the reason, the substitute's name and whether she has posted all of this information into her payroll book.

During this process, the phone has rung eight times, three with messages, one asking if there is any school today, and four parental call-in's regarding student's absences. She has answered the school intercom, which has a beeping sound. Each teacher has a button in their room which is their access to the office. One teacher wants the secretary to tell another teacher that a certain student is on his way to the other teacher's room. The intercom is to be used for emergencies only! Sometimes the staff has a tendency to forget the rule.

Back to the payroll. She marks all the appropriate spots and puts it in the folder marked "Action Items" and places it in the middle of the principal's desk for his signature. It needs to be in the school mail by 2:30 p.m. The school has finished up their ITBS tests and are in the process of making up tests for those students who were not in attendance. The principal calls down the students on the intercom and takes them across the hall to the auditorium. The secretary sorts through the returned answer sheets to make sure everyone gridded their names and serial numbers in the proper places. She finds two whole classes who right justified instead of left justified. The aide helps erase and they enter them correctly.

The phone rings and it is an irate parent upset with the bus driver for stopping the bus until everyone on the bus was quiet. Her child arrived late for school and missed breakfast, and what were we going to do about it. The secretary gives the parent the number of the bus barn and asks her to talk with them regarding the bus driver.

When the principal comes through to use the intercom, the

secretary tells him about the irate parent along with two other phone messages.

It's recess time and several children come in with skinned knees, one has thrown up on the playground. The secretary takes care of the skinned knees, the aide handles the upset stomach. The two work very compatibly together. The aide can't handle blood, the secretary can't handle upset stomachs.

The secretary receives a call from another school in the district. They have enrolled four of her students, would she please send the records. She gives them their student numbers and writes their names down in her enrollment "bible" -- This is the book the secretary keeps all of the "in students" and "out students" names in and a record of whether their reading folder, immunization card and student folder was sent or received. Earlier that morning she had entered the names of the three new students who had enrolled and from the area they were last enrolled. The attendance aide also uses this book to keep the attendance records up to date.

This particular elementary secretary works in a highly mobile, inner-city average size school with a population of about 500 students. Some elementary secretaries will state they have a lot of movement if they displace 30-50 students in a year. This particular school will displace itself one and a half times during the school year. Many hours of the secretary's time will be spent on the in's and out's and the handling of student records. She has a marvelous reading specialist, nurse (when she's scheduled in the building), aide and principal, who work as a team. It cannot be done alone, only through great cooperation from all parts of the team.

Needless to say, the rest of the day will run a similar course as the morning with one exception. The nurse is scheduled in the afternoon, and the aide goes home.

I cannot say enough about the diversity of an elementary secretary's position. She has to be the jack-of-all-trades and master them all. She carries a wealth of information in her head, which only comes from experience on the job.

Problems

Let's get down to the basic problems of the elementary secretary. You can all relate to the typical day. Now, what can we do to help you or improve your day. In giving workshops throughout the United States, I always ask the participants to write down their one major problem. I either ask them to write down the level they work and/or divide them into sections.

Here are some of the typical responses:

- ---Interruptions
- ---Distribution of work load
- ---Communication
- ---Phone interruption
- ---Lack of Communication
- ---No time to learn new equipment
- ---Last minute jobs which could be avoided
- ---Too much work
- ---Telephone rings too much
- ---Telephone calls from parents
- ---Lack of communication between boss and secretary
- ---Need another phone extension--and intercom button at my desk
- ---Inadequate, non-working, outdated equipment
- ---Non-stop details
- ---Too many jobs to do, too many interruptions
- ---Everyone not working together
- ---Major responsibilities occur at same time each year so I cannot make the workload flow smoothly
- ---Workload
- ---Morale
- ---Old equipment
- ---Not enough help. Teachers expect too much
- ---Too many tasks, all at one time, telephone, selling, lunch orders
- ---Everything ends up on the counter, teachers don't put away what they get out.
- ---Too much work, not enough time.
- ---Work distribution
- ---Getting everything done
- ---Not always knowing where my boss is, out of the office a lot.
- ---Being uninformed
- ---Shortage of time/interruptions

As you look through the listing you should be able to relate to many of the problems. The three that get repeated more than any of the others are: the lack of communication, interruptions, too much to do!

After I ask them to write down their number one problem, I ask what they can do about the problem. A lot of times the answer is *nothing*. So, let's talk about the answers to the problems of elementary secretaries.

Solutions

Let me quickly jot down some of the suggested solutions by elementary secretaries.

They suggested:
- ---Be courteous, but proceed with work
- ---Be calm
- ---Request a meeting to discuss the lack of communication.
- ---Try to get my job description changed (I love this one!)
- ---We've asked for more input, but sometimes we get help, but mostly nothing is done.
- ---Ask more questions
- ---Attend more staff meetings (include secretaries)
- ---Ask for communication ahead of time, don't expect co-workers to read your mind.
- ---Be positive / open to change
- ---Have a positive attitude, be tactfully honest
- ---Learn ways to effectively communicate
- ---Communicate and *prod*
- ---Be positive, be open to change, perhaps personal & professional development
- ---Make changes where possible
- ---Be authoritive, time management
- ---Be more organized, and divide up tasks for different times
- ---Complete one task before beginning another
- ---Need time for training
- ---Parent calls--we've tried asking them to give instructions by a note to the teacher, when the children come to school
- ---Bite my tongue
- ---Cope
- ---Do the best possible job, and try to keep a positive attitude
- ---Extra help and / or better organization
- ---Keep trying, learn to manage stress
- ---Talk about the problems
- ---Keep informed and up to date with new secretarial ideas
- ---Continually educate and keep secretaries informed on changes in our field
- ---Keep requesting new machines - perserverance wins

---Ask the boss to give her a schedule of his day
---Try to be more open and assertive
---Try to stay organized

Just look at all of the great solutions that can be found when the question is asked - "what can you do to help solve your problem?" Some solutions are simple, others have to be given a little more thought and a little more time.

The major over all bandaid that will cover most of the problems will be your involvement in communication. You have to be able to convey what your problem involves to the person that can help solve the problem. If your problem involves the organization of your time, then it will have to be solved within your parameters. Reorganize your time schedule, renew your faith in time management or anything that will help you feel comfortable in your position.

With the limitation on financing in education today the possibility of a full time nurse and / or additional aides to help in elementary offices seems far from becoming a reality. We can write another whole chapter on the liability of administering medication, on discipline in the office, and on decision making. In fact, we could write a complete book on the elementary secretary. As I stated in the beginning, the elementary secretary is a unique person.

One of most important parts in the puzzle of education is the fact that we are, many times, the first person a child, a parent, a visitor, sees and meets when they first enter a school building. How we treat the people on the other side of the office counter will long be remembered by that child, that parent or that visitor. We need to remember that we are the public relations officer for our school. We need to smile at the child who comes in with the skinned knee and give sympathy where it's needed. No matter how busy the phones become, no matter how many times the intercom buzzes, no matter how many reports you are trying to fill out, you still need to treat the people on the other side of the counter like human beings.

I have not said much about the Principal / Secretary relationship. Maybe it's because I have an excellent team relationship in my building. You notice how possessive elementary secretaries become, it's MY building! My administrator gives me latitude to make decisions that affect the workload in my office, yet I know the fine line which runs between being a secretary and being the administrator. The administrator is responsible for the total building program, my responsibility lies within the framework of my office.

It is very important to have a good line of open communication between the Principal and Secretary. If you do not have that openess, then you need to sit down with your administrator and talk about the problem. If that doesn't work, you can only hope he will retire soon, transfer to another school or district. I am serious when I say, you need to be able to wake up in the morning and be happy about going to your job. If you are not, then you need to re-evaluate your whole lifestyle and then you need to change your attitude about your work, you need to transfer to another school, or retire. That probably sounds a little hard, but on the other hand, there is nothing worse than someone who is in a position they are unhappy in and do nothing but complain and grump to the children. Regardless of the makeup of an elementary building, it should be a happy place for children to go to school.

Relationships are more important than things! Everyday something will change, nothing ever stays the same. The key to your day will be communication. Those three things are important rules that will play a part in your everyday schedule. How we treat one another is more important than the new typewriter, although it does rank right up there with a new copy machine. The only one that we can change is ourselves. We can change how we accept others and how we accept the daily changes in our lives. We cannot change other people, only our acceptance of other people.

In closing, there will never be enough hours in the day for an elementary secretary. You need to adjust to the fact that when you think you have everything done, there will be another job to fill that void, and another, and another. You try to get done each day what is physically and mentally posible, make your list for the next day, and go home, satisfied that you have given it your best shot.

You need to know there are solutions to your problems. Common sense will tell you what they are. We all know how to solve problems. Look at the listing those elementary secretaries were able to come up with, all on their own, nobody helped them think it through, the answers are always there. Take the time to think your problem through and you'll come up with a good elementary common sense approach to the problem and you'll also feel good about the solution.

John Holladay, a noted artist, in his less noted days, drew a pencil sketch of me with my foot in a file drawer, the telephone propped up to my ear, I was typing a letter, answering a teacher, all at the same time. It's kind of significant, that as a teacher, that was how he perceived the secretary. It does kind of explain an elementary secretary's position and I love every minute of it!!

chapter sixteen
the effective assistant principal's secretary

By: Sarah Clapp

Who doesn't mind constantly ringing telephones? Who braves the wilds of complaining parents with concern? Who can teachers unload their curriculum/class complaints and feel like they have really been heard? The Assistant Principal's secretary; the person any one from parent to custodian from teacher and student (and sometimes the Assistant Principal himself) feels they can seek out for "the right answer."

The Assistant Principal's secretary is actually the Assistant Principal of the school (to a great extent but don't tell the AP). She controls the meeting schedule, initially handles problems, initiates research on problems and complaints so the AP can put the final action in motion. The only thing the AP secretary does not share with the AP is salary and the final decisions affecting the school. And there are even times the AP does not have the final say - it's the high school principal. The AP secretary really is his administrative assistant, support team for those harrowing days, and his cheerleader when he has that great idea for the Master Schedule or room assignment, etc. She buffs the complaints from teachers, parents and students.

The AP secretary is a "girl Friday" in all reality. The job entails knowing the school staff and facilities in conjunction with community needs. She covers for the principal's secretary when she's out, may be called upon to assist in the counseling department, can usually fix ditto and copy machines, and when there are VIP's on campus, is called upon to make sure the school image is at its best.

Of course, all this is contingent upon the AP's job responsibilities, but for the most part, your AP is the Principal's "right hand man" and trouble shoots for him, prepares preliminary reports, etc.

Generally, the AP secretary is a regular secretary, she sets up meetings, screens telephone calls, types reports and memos, keeps a watchful eye on the calendar (and clock), and keeps track of ALL correspondence.

My experience comes from the AP job description within our Palm Springs Unified School District. Let's take a look at what my AP actually does.

ASSISTANT PRINCIPAL, CURRICULUM AND INSTRUCTION

Principal Designee #1	Problem Analysis
Research & Planning	Staff Development
Curriculum	Master Scheduling
Instruction	Alternative Programs
Articulation	Testing
Counseling and Guidance	Learning Proficiencies
Career Center	Graduation Requirements
Budget Planning & Implementation	Instructional Media (Library)
Registration	Contract Management
Academic Records	Special Projects
Evaluation:	Driver Training
Personnel	Substitutes
Programs	Gifted/Talented Program
Services	Bilingual Program
	Academic Departments
	(Supervision/Coordination)

In referring to the AP job responsibilities, this is how my day operates in conjunction with my supervisor.

My workday starts with checking the AP's calendar against my own. I update for both calendars to match and, if it appears the AP has an unusually busy day scheduled, I type his appointments on a 3x5 card for him to carry and refer to throughout the day. I then grab a cup of coffee, check with the Principal's secretary to update deadlines, reports, appointments that need to be added or deleted for the day, etc. If the Principal is not in the office for the day, I know the majority of phone requests and problem solving will affect our office and try to adjust the day for more flexibility. I review the school's daily bulletin and note anything the AP should be particularly aware of; i.e. duty schedule, activities on campus, etc.

I do my best work early in the morning so I then move into my dictation and get the typing out of the way. All of this has been left on my desk the evening before by my supervisor. We keep everything in a folder we pass back and forth since most of the work is confidential. Once typed, the material moves to a "Review / Sign" folder that later in the morning the AP checks over, signs and I receive back for mailing and distribution. Incoming mail is reviewed in the early afternoon and the AP responds to the correspondence in the latter part of the day. I do my filing immediately (when mail is prepared and copies have been made). I find this does not allow filing to pile up, and it's where the AP can find the information easily. Filing is a tedious job but when you stay on top of it, it never becomes a "job"; it's always caught up.

After my initial morning correspondence, I move along to the long-term typing projects (reports, emergency memos, etc.). I have a word processor so drafts of reports or lengthy memos can be easily restructured.

A lot of material I generate is "survey" in nature and is to be returned (to yours truly). When doing a lot of surveys, class lists and signed evaluations are being generated at one time, I use colored paper for ease in sorting out the results. Also, the paperwork that is more time related (senior fail notices, for example, are tabulated as they hit the tray. I keep a separate tray for just this "to be returned" paperwork.

The *telephone*. It rings often, and is usually of a complaint or "I don't know where else to turn" type of call. Try to receive all phone calls with a smile in your voice and screen as best you can. I always inform the caller that the AP is not available but, being secretary, I can take the initial information (and emphasize that anything relayed will remain confidential if that is the case) and the AP will research before he returns their call. This saves your AP time, and I have found that most of the initial research can actually be done by me so all the AP has to do is follow up and finalize. If it is a teacher related complaint, you might want to keep a tally for your AP; especially if several parents are responding to a particular class situation.

Try to convey to your caller that their message is the most important thing you have to do right now and will receive your top priority. It leaves a positive impression of the school and the person will end the call thinking how much the school and district really cares about what they have to say and has the student's best interest in mind. VERY IMPORTANT. We are a people business - and those people need to know that we think they are number one. I have had parents call and not want to leave much of a message for fear their own student will find out they are complaining or obtaining information for a school function. That's when you turn the call into a "parent to parent" call, assuring them they obviously have their student's best interest at heart and how reassuring it is that they care to ask.

Positive school atmosphere needs to be constantly conveyed and the telephone is your #1 spot for public relations. If *you* care that means the *AP* cares, which means the *school* cares, etc.

I end my day with doing "odds and ends" tasks, anything that the AP has placed on my desk that isn't "right now" but "take care of soon" material. I do my survey telephoning after school is over for the day so I can sit and properly field questions with other schools in a relaxed manner; there are less people trying to get my attention, plus the person on the other end of the phone is also finished with the hustle and bustle of students in their day and they can sit and respond as well.

The AP and I try to find a space of time, even if it's a three minute time slot where we are able to touch base and check on things that are being done. How about that long term survey project? Have I started the Board of Ed report and what is my time estimate for completion? This helps you keep on top of things and at the same time assist the AP in thinking through obligations and responsibilities. Many times in these type of meetings new ideas have come to light or something is brought up that can be added to assist with that "special report."

The telephone message book I use for the AP has been most helpful. I record all messages, phone numbers and names in one book with a space for response. When the AP has returned a call and/or taken action for the call, he notates it out to the side. This book is returned to me, enabling me to know what has been done, if the call has been returned, etc. This set-up has been very handy when we have been accused of "not following through" for the proof is on the paper what was done. Great back-up!!

Original Folder. I have made up a lot of forms and procedures that are used time and again for opening school day, open house, grading procedures, etc., and forms for the counseling department. The main message here is *keep your original.* You will find after two years or so you will be pulling and referring to these originals that may just need a section changed, something reworded or may be deleted altogether. It is easy to go straight to your Originals File and make the adjustment and it's on the way in no time. Saves you lots of retyping time and you look efficient!

The bottom line to being a good and effective AP secretary is TRUST in working with your AP. It builds over time as long as you don't betray that trust, you keep the best interest of the school, and don't ever release a confidentiality, you will work for the greatest person around. The AP is growing in his profession to someday be a high school principal - which enables you to grow in your secretarial position to better ideas for the office, school, etc. AP's are encouragers, and will run the extra mile for you and the school. It's the best job to have as long as you maintain a sense of humor and take everything with a grain of salt.

chapter seventeen
the effective higher education secretary

By: Jackie Fuller, CEOE

INTRODUCTION

An effective higher education secretary is one who can keep 15 jobs going at once while remaining calm and collected; who is able to juggle an endless list of job assignments from multiple bosses and manage to get them done when requested; and who not only knows her own job well but is also knowledgeable of the university system in which she works. This secretary must be flexible, must not mind constant interruptions, and above all, must enjoy people.

Jobs within a university setting vary. You may find yourself working in the office of an administrator such as a College Dean, the Director of the physical plant, or the University Librarian. You may work in a service office like the Registrar's Office where you would deal with students and maintain student records, or you may be a departmental secretary. In the case of the service-type department, you may work for one or two supervisors and many peers. In contrast, in the departmental office, you would likely be the only secretary working for several professors as well as the Department Chairman. (Some departments have as many as 40 faculty members!) Whatever the position you hold, be aware that an office employee in higher education is an extremely important person to the institution she serves. This chapter will explore some methods that will help you become a more effective higher-education secretary.

BEING EFFECTIVE ON THE JOB

Welcoming Office Visitors

In the majority of cases, the secretary is the first person visitors meet upon entering an office. Because of this initial contact, the impression others have of your unit depends upon you. Always keep in mind that a positive image and a professional manner make people more comfortable. In many university offices, the majority of the office visitors will be students who will enter your office for a myriad of reasons. Students may ask questions about the major requirements of the departmental program(s). Although you are not an academic advisor--the professors in your department have this responsibility--you still should learn all you can about the program(s). Keeping up to date on major requirements will enable you to answer many of the routine questions. You will not only save your bosses another interruption, but you will also save the student some time.

Students will also enter your office to ask questions about university rules, regulations, and policies. Often students drop in because they don't know where else to go and your office happens to be handy. They need help, so the last thing they want to hear is "I don't know." As an effective educational secretary, you should be able to answer these questions or be able to direct the student to the office that can be of help.

The manner in which you approach a student can mean the difference between his continuing with his career plans or giving up school altogether because he did not receive the help he needed from an office worker who wouldn't take the time to find out the answer or who gave the impression of not caring. Being able to answer his questions or to direct him properly, may be just what he needed at the time--a friendly, helpful, and efficient secretary. Just imagine the affect you may have on the life of this student.

As a higher-education secretary, you should never be heard to say "I sure wish these students would leave me alone," or "I could sure get more work done if the students would quit interrupting me." If you ever have thoughts like these, you may want to remind yourself that without the students, your job would not exist. Someone stated it so well when he wrote the following:

THE STUDENT IS

... the most important person on the campus. Without students there would be no need for the institution.

... not a cold enrollment statistic but a flesh and blood human being with feelings and emotions like our own.

... not someone to be tolerated so that we can do our thing. They are our thing.

... not dependent on us. Rather, we are dependent on them.

... not an interruption of our work, but the purpose of it. We are not doing them a favor by serving them. They are doing us a favor by giving us the opportunity to do so.

---Anonymous

LEARNING YOUR JOB

The main thing you must do when you take a job as a higher education secretary is to learn your job well. Not only is it imperative for you to learn your duties well, but you should also become familiar with the duties and functions of the people you work for. You will learn many of these responsibilities as your bosses assign work. Pay attention to these jobs and you will gain a lot of useful information. However, the efficient secretary doesn't stop there.

One thing you can do to increase your knowledge quickly is to become familiar with the files, forms, and manuals that are in your office. Within the first few months of your new job, take a few minutes each day to look through the files. By reviewing the files, you can find out what letter style is preferred, what forms are used, and what type of reports and manuscripts that have been typed by the previous secretary. When you are given similar work, you will already be familiar with the materials needed and will know exactly where to find what you need in the files. Seeing how forms and other documents were done (for instance, what margins were used) can be very helpful.

If your institution is like most, you will probably find an entire file drawer devoted to blank forms. Plan to review these forms before you ever have to use them--perhaps one a day. Notice what information is required, who must fill the form out and why, and what signatures are needed. You will gain a lot of useful information from this study. When a co-worker or a student asks you for a particular form (often by the wrong name) you will not only know just where to look for it but will be able answer questions regarding this form.

Learning all facets of your job may take as long as one year because many tasks in higher education offices occur only once or twice a year. For example, you may be responsible for ordering the text books needed each semester through the campus bookstore. The deadline for fall orders is--say, March 15. Once you have typed the forms and sent them off, you will not repeat this duty again untill October when spring orders are due; then again next March. Determining which faculty members will march at the graduation ceremonies and typing annual evaluations of each faculty member in your department are once-a-year jobs. As you can see, the higher education secretary has a wide variety of duties that occur infrequently. Instead of waiting to be assigned these tasks, the effective secretary learns to anticipate what is to come and to do some preliminary work when she has time.

How can this efficient secretary remember all of these infrequent duties?

Recurring Duties Log

A good plan is to maintain a "Recurring Duties" log for all re-occurring jobs. Develop a series of 12 folders—one for each month. Inside each folder maintain a page with five columns—one for each week. (See example on next page).

In each column, write the duties that occur that week each year. For example, if book orders are due on March 15 each year, enter "book orders due" in the second column of the March recurring duties form. If the graduation list is due April 1, enter "graduation participation list due April 1" in the last column of the March sheet. Separate each entry by a line across the column.

RECURRING DUTIES

Month _____

Week Beginning	Week Beginning	Week Beginning	Week Beginning	Week Beginning
_____	_____	_____	_____	_____

Use a pencil so entries can be erased and moved if due dates or responsibilities change.

In each folder, keep supporting documentation to show you how each duty was done the last time. For instance, you might keep a copy of the memo you sent to faculty asking which books they planned to adopt in the March folder. In the April folder, you would keep a list of the faculty who participated in the graduation ceremony the previous year so you will know whose turn it is the next year. A copy of a completed faculty evaluation would be handy to help you remember the format used the previous year. Official copies of all documents, of course, are filed in the appropriate place in your office-the copies in your Recurring Duties file are just for your information and efficiency.

Mark your calendar on the first day of each month to remind yourself to retrieve the folder for that month. Look it over to see what things you will be doing that month. Keep in mind that not all of your duties are listed here--only the ones that occur once or twice throughout the year. Other duties will be assigned and completed as requested.

If you are new to a position, develop the "recurring duties" list during your first year by entering each week's duties as you work through the year. If you have been on the job a while, you could probably complete the list all at once and refine it as you use it. A good source of due dates may be your institution's Administrative Handbook. These hand books frequently list due dates for information to be sent to the central administration each year.

In the event that you have slack time, look ahead to see if you can begin any of the projects that are on your "recurring duties" list. When your boss says, "We need to determine who will be marching in the graduation ceremonies this year" you will be able to say, "Oh, I have already typed up the list and here it is." Do this a few times and your boss will be extremely pleased and impressed with you!

There certainly will be times when you will wonder if you ever will be able to complete all of your assignments, but don't panic. Just make a list of all of the things you have to do, continue to work on them one at a time, and cross off each item as it is completed. The sense of satisfaction you will derive from crossing each one off the list will give you a lift. Here are a few hints that may help you increase your efficiency.

Work Request Form

If you work for several bosses, you may want to design a "Work Request Form" to be filled in by each person making an assignment. Include a space on the form to describe the assignment and list a series of items to be checked off such as number of copies needed, whether the document is a draft or final copy, and if it is to be collated and stapled. Most importantly, include a place to fill in the due date. (See example on next page.) This form not only helps you keep your work organized, it saves the time it would take for interruptions by bosses requesting work.

The efficient secretary, especially one who works for many bosses, will always try to complete a project several days before the due date on the work request. Waiting until the due date is too risky. Plan to complete each assignment at least two days before the due date--provided your bosses cooperate by giving you several days lead time on each assignment. If they don't, ask them for more lead time because, to have an efficiently run office, everyone must cooperate. By allowing yourself two days leeway, you have a buffer in case you have to call in sick or a power outage keeps you from working on your projects. When you are sick with the flu, it isn't much fun to have to come to work because you had not yet typed a test due to be administered to a class later that day. And you may make others in the office feel guilty for asking you to come in, even though it is your fault for putting off the job until the due date!

Use of Colored Folders

How do you keep track of the many projects you must complete? Are they in a single stack that you must go through each time you are ready for a new project? Or are they segregated into separate folders? Can you tell by looking at the stack of folders what is in each one without looking through each one? You may want to try the following time saving suggestion.

File folders come in many bright colors. You may not want to go to the expense of using these folders in your files, but do get some for organizing the work on your desk. Colored file folders work very well for keeping assignments sorted out and for fast retrieval. Give each colored file a specific purpose. For example:

WORK REQUEST

To: (Sec.) _____ Date: _____

From: _____ Course #: _____ Date Needed _____

_____ Typing: _____ Draft _____ Final

_____ Test Security

_____ Xerox: _____ # Copies

_____ Collate _____ Staple

_____ Punch _____ 2-Hole _____ 3-Hole

_____ File Original

_____ File Copy

Instructions / Corrections _____

_____

_____

_____

_____

_____

_____

_____

NOTE: Material submitted with less than <u>five</u> working days preparation time cannot be guaranteed!!!!

Green	Short, easily done assignments such as letters, memos, forms, and other one- to two-page documents
Brown	A long research paper
Orange	All budget papers that must be posted to the books and / or filed
Yellow	Test and classroom materials
Blue	Filing
Pink	Projects that must be duplicated / photocopied

The rest of the colors--Purple, Grey, White--can be used for infrequent projects such as book orders and class schedules. When all of these colored folders are in your work tray on your desk, you can readily find the project you want to work on next because of the color. Using these folders saves time that would have been spent looking through several manila folders to find the one you want.

The "Green" Folder. As small assignments come in during the day, file them in your green folder. Since these assignments take the least amount of time to complete, do them the first thing each morning. Clear everything out of this green folder before you progress to the other major projects. The remainder of the day, as small assignments come in, file them in the green folder for the next day.

The "Red" Folder. Red folders are the most noticeable. Use these folders for completed assignments that require your boss' signature. On the outside of the red folders, type a label that says, "FOR YOUR SIGNATURE." Your boss is sure to notice the folder on his desk and will get these items back to you faster because they are not as likely to get buried in a stack of other items on the desk.

Scheduling Meetings

Finding a given time that an entire group of people can meet can be one of the most time-consuming assignments you will have. Faculty and staff at a college or university attend numerous meetings, many with representatives from a number of campus departments and offices. Faculty are very busy people and, of course, teach classes at different hours throughout the day. If you are asked to find a time that is convenient for eight committee members to meet and to schedule a meeting during that time, you could spend hours on the telephone. Finding everyone in their offices when you make your calls is not probable and when you have finally contacted each one and found out that a time you thought would work does not, it is back to the phone to call each one again! Sounds familiar, doesn't it?

Next time, try this. Develop a form that has a weekly grid of class times used at your institution. There should be a space for each class hour on each day of the week--Monday through Friday. (See example on next page.) When your boss asks you to find a convenient meeting time for a certain week, send a copy of this form to each committee member with a memo attached giving the following instruction: "Mark out all of the times that you are NOT available for a meeting of the ----- committee during the week of March 17-21. Return the form to me by March 13."

When all of the forms are returned, use a blank form to mark out all of the times blocked out on each of the committee members' forms. If there are any blank spaces, schedule your meeting during one of those times. Call each committee member to tell them when the meeting is or you can leave a message because you know he is available at that hour. Of course, there may not be any blank spaces on your master form. In that case, discuss it with your boss. He should be the one to make the decision on who to leave out or whether to schedule the meeting during another week.

Working for Multiple Bosses

Working for multiple bosses isn't easy. The biggest problem is that each one is unaware of the jobs the others have already assigned to you. They have no way of knowing that you already have eight 60-question multiple choice tests to type, duplicate, collate, and staple, as well as 14 letters of recommendation, a 23-page research paper to type, and the budget to reconcile.

Mark out all of the times that you are <u>not</u> available
for a meeting of the
_____ committee during the week of _____

	Monday	Wednesday	Friday		Tuesday	Thursday
7:40				7:40		
8:30						
8:40				8:55		
9:30				9:15		
9:40						
10:30				10:30		
10:40				10:40		
11:30						
11:40				11:55		
12:30				12:15		
12:40						
1:30				1:30		
1:40				1:40		
2:30						
2:40				2:55		
3:30				3:15		
3:40						
4:30				4:30		

You also have a list of other odd jobs that must be completed by the next day! But even if they did know all that you have to do, their work is still important and must be done. The key is flexibility.

Don't expect to come to work in the morning, look at your assignments, and say to yourself, "I am going to get this, this, and this done today." Your work load can be changed within the hour by being given a job that is more pressing. You were certainly right to prioritize your work, but be flexible enough to change the priority order often.

Other Efficient Management Techniques

There are numerous ways a secretary can become more efficient. Constantly be on the lookout for new management ideas. Your university library has a multitude of office manuals as well as books and magazines about time management, telephone techniques, and secretarial aids. Take advantage of your privileges as a staff member within the institution; check out some of these books.

Most institutions will also allow staff members to attend university classes by waiving fees or offering them at a reduced rate. You may be able to take a class during working hours if it is job related. Look into this possibility at your school and sign up for a class if you can. Your boss might even pay your way to a job-related workshop if you tell him you are interested in upgrading your skills.

Maintaining Confidentiality

The tests you type for the faculty are confidential and must be kept secure at all times. If you are interrupted while typing and must be away from your desk even for a short while, put the exam away. Though it is unpleasant to admit it, there are some students who will do anything to get their hands on an advance copy of a test. You may even have someone offer you money for a copy. Be sure you have a good security system for maintaining your test files and refrain from labelling those file drawers!

A tremendous amount of material you work with in a higher-education office will be confidential in nature. You will type the chairman's evaluations of your faculty, handle student evaluations of faculty members, and know each faculty's annual salary. You will also have access to all types of student records including transcripts, probation and dismissal lists, and grade sheets. You must be careful not to discuss any of this information with your friends, co-workers, or students. As a matter of fact, due to the Family Educational Rights Privacy Act of 1974, you can't even discuss a student's grades with her mother without her permission!

The effective secretary takes to heart the word that is made from the first six letters of the word "secretary."

LEARNING ABOUT THE INSTITUTION

In a higher education setting, just knowing your job well does not necessarily make you an effective secretary. It is also important to know the functions of the university as a whole. The more you know about the entire campus and how you and your department fit into the total picture, the more effective you will be in your job. You will be able to answer questions for students, faculty, and other office visitors--as well as for your boss--even though their questions may be out of your normal realm. You will soon see how much your help will be appreciated.

Where to start? There are many publications that are extremely helpful in gaining knowledge of the entire academic system.

Organizational Chart

First of all, obtain a copy of the institution's organizational chart. This chart will show the chain of command for the university. First, locate your department on the chart. Follow the line to the next step. This will show the person (or department) that your boss reports to. If you work for an academic department, this person will most likely be the Dean of the College. Follow the line to the next step. You will see that the dean probably reports to the Academic Vice President or Executive Vice President. You will find that this person reports to the President.

If you check one of the many forms used in your department regarding academic affairs, you will notice that the signatures required on the form follow this same line of command. Now you know why! Forms dealing with budgetary items may require the signatures of the department head, dean, and then the Budget Director and Financial Vice President. Study the chart to see why. Knowing the organizational chart can be invaluable to you when you require some information or when you must direct a person to a certain office.

University Catalog (or Bulletin)

Every college and university publishes a "catalog" or "bulletin." This book contains information about the university and its services. You will find student information about admission requirements, fees and expenses, student housing, and student services. Also listed are requirements for every major field, descriptions of courses taught, requirements for graduation, and an array of other information. The answers to most of the questions students ask can be found in this publication. The student is given a copy when he enters school and he should be familiar with its contents. However, students often don't read it. Don't make the same mistake. Take time to familiarize yourself with this valuable book. Don't read the entire book; just look through it so you are aware of its contents. Then, if you need an answer, you will know where to find it. However, do become knowledgeable about your own department's section of the book. You must know this information.

Student Handbook

Another important source of student information is the Student Handbook. Much of the information in this handbook is also printed in the Catalog but the handbook contains other information as well. There is usually a section of general information--where to get help, where to park, and services provided for the students on campus. The book details what a student must do if she or he wants to drop one class or wants to drop out of school entirely. Though these are similar requests, they may be handled by entirely different offices. And the effective higher education secretary knows this information. The Student Handbook tells students that the university has offices for financial aid, career planning and placement, personal counseling, and a student health service. Information about the library is also given. The handbook will tell a student how to become active in student government, university committees, and other student organizations. An efficient secretary has learned from the handbook where students can go to make room and board payments, to pick up an on-campus paycheck, to get a copy of their transcript, to drop a class, to apply for graduation, to get tutoring, to file a grievance, or to join student government.

By the way, your department faculty will often ask you for the same information. Keep a copy of this handbook handy!

Faculty and Administrative Handbooks

The faculty will also want information on policies that affect them. Two important handbooks you will want to peruse are the Faculty Handbook and the Administrative Handbook. The Faculty Handbook contains information on such policies as promotion, tenure, travel, committees, and sabbatical leaves. The Administrative Handbook includes these policies as well as ones that affect the entire university. This book is where you will find the organizational chart and the list of due dates mentioned earlier. Make yourself familiar with these handbooks; learn how to look up information quickly. Your boss should also be familiar with these policies, but he will learn to rely on you if you show him you have done your homework! You may earn valuable points when evaluation time comes along!

Schedule of Classes

Also you should thoroughly know the information contained in the Schedule of Classes. This book is published each semester or quarter and lists the classes offered that term. It contains a wealth of information that is important to students and faculty alike. By the number of inquiries you get, you will think that no one ever reads it! As well as the class listings showing times and places, the schedule contains a calendar of important dates and registration information, a final exam schedule, and other useful information. Flip through it-you will be glad you did!

Discover the Campus

Now that you have studied all of the publications and have become familiar with what goes on at your campus, it is time to see *where* it is going on!

It is extremely useful to know where--or at least the general vicinity--each office on campus is located. Directing visitors to these areas is so much easier if you have been there. Besides, it is fun to see the entire campus and to meet the other people who work there.

First, acquire a campus map. (You should know exactly where to get one because several of the above mentioned books that you have studied contain one.) Then plan a few lunch hour sojourns in different directions each time you go out. See where the buildings are and learn their names. Find out which offices are in each building. If you have time, walk through the buildings noting just where these departments are. You may even want to use your breaks in this way. You will not only learn the layout of the campus, but you will get some exercise as well!

CONCLUSION

Working as an office employee in an institution of higher education can be a rewarding experience. The variety of assignments keeps the job from getting boring, and the secretary has a chance to meet a wide variety of people. The person holding this type of job must work constantly to improve the efficiency of her unit and, in doing so, will soon become an EFFECTIVE HIGHER EDUCATION SECRETARY.